Let's Schmooze:
Jewish Words Today

LET'S SCHMOOZE
Jewish Words
Today

Rabbi Julian Sinclair

continuum

Continuum
The Tower Building, 11 York Road, London SE1 7NX
80 Maiden Lane, Suite 704, New York, NY 10038

www.continuumbooks.com

British Library Cataloguing-in-Publication Data
A catalogue record for this book is available from the British Library.

082649711X

Typeset by BookEns Ltd, Royston, Herts.
Printed and bound by MPG Books Ltd, Bodmin, Cornwall

Contents

Introduction

I first became interested in Jewish words when I married a Jewish girl from Brooklyn. My wife is third-generation American, from an Ivy League school and fluent in Yiddish. She learned the basics from her grandfather, a native speaker, took a couple of courses in college and now she can *schmooze* with anyone in the *ganze oilam*.

I began to feel that I'd missed out. Not just me, but my parents and grandparents too. It would drive my wife *meshuggah* when they'd misuse or mispronounce the handful of Yiddish words they did know, *schlepping* (instead of *schepping*) *naches* from their grandchildren, as if the satisfaction their offspring provided was extraordinarily burdensome.

Gradually, I learned how my birthright had been stolen from me in exchange for a thin gruel of Anglo-Jewry gentility. I discovered the story of how the masses of Eastern European immigrants to Britain in between 1880–1920 were acculturated with ruthless efficiency by the West End Anglo-Jewish establishment, anxious about

1

what a lot of uncouth foreigners would do to their standing in British society. A whole network of Anglicizing institutions sprang up around the turn of the twentieth century, from the Jews' Free School to the Jewish Lads' and Girls' Brigade, all bent on inculcating English manners, discipline and etiquette, literature, history and geography, as well as forbidding the utterance of a single word of Yiddish. No doubt there was a modicum of disinterested benevolence in all this philanthropy, but there was a hefty element of communal control too, 'designed to protect the status of the communal elite at the expense of the culture of the communal poor', as the historian Bill Williams put it.[1]

Israel Zangwill expressed the spirit of the time, in this ditty (originally composed in Yiddish):

> My brothers and sisters newly here,
> Listen to my wise oration.
> You can live without the fear
> Of hatred or repatriation.
> All you have to do, I bid,
> Is stop acting like a yid.
>
> *Ei, ei, ei* is so demeaning,
> English voices sing so sweet,

---

[1] Bill Williams, 'East and West in Manchester Jewry', in David Cesarani (ed.) *The Making of Modern Anglo-Jewry*, (Oxford, 1990).

Ei, ei, ei, is so demeaning
Oi, Oi, Oi, an ugly bleat.
Pom, pom, pom, is rude and crazy,
Try instead 'tra lah' or 'daisy'.

Chorus:
Yes, we would love to be MPs
And we will learn to do all this.
We will say, 'how do you please',
And cultivate communal bliss.
We will change our ways and struggle,
To eat our Christmas pudding right,
Put away our Yiddish *kugel*,
Read our Milton every night.
We will call Rev. Adler 'chief',
And nobody will come to grief.[2]

The experiment in social engineering succeeded magnificently. Within a couple of decades, British Jewry had reared a new generation who were constitutionally incapable of saying '*oy, oy, oy*' but stood in the front row at the Proms, and although they couldn't make head nor tail of a page of Talmud, they knew the England batting averages by heart.

My generation growing up in the 1970s and 1980s

---

[2] Israel Zangwill, 'Quoted without source in Howard Cooper and Paul Morrison, *A Sense of Belonging* (London, 1991) 76–7.

knew that the ersatz anglicized Judaism of our parents somehow lacked the real *geshmack*. Many of us understandably drifted further away from Anglo-Jewishness, but some tried to retrace our grandparents' steps back towards more authentic brands of *Yiddishkeit*. Throughout the community there was a renaissance of Jewish learning from the Orthodox Project Seed to the cross-denominational Limmud conference. Secular Jewish identity bloomed too, through literature, drama and music. Oxford University became an unlikely fountainhead of Yiddish language and culture.

From the 1970s onwards one could pursue these journeys under the flag of convenience of multiculturalism. Monolithic Englishness was crumbling, and gradually it became acceptable to be British and something else. Not yet the effortlessly hyphenated identity of Jewish-Americans, but nevertheless Jews took their place among the ranks of recognized ethnic minorities in whom our post-imperial British hosts began to display a belated curiosity.

True, it took some time to realize that the multicultural dispensation applied equally to Jews. While Arundati Roy hooked the Booker Prize, Jewish fiction was still being rejected by (often Jewish) agents and publishers as 'too Jewish', perhaps because our grandparents did such an excellent job of presenting British Jewry as thoroughly mainstream and boring. But with Naomi Alderman now being touted by Penguin as the Jewish Zadie Smith, and her Orthodox north-west London milieu described on the jacket blurbs as 'exotic', it seems that the cat is at long last out of the bag: in many ways Jews are jolly odd. And to my grandmother's surprise and relief, public realization of this fact is leading not to Zangwill's feared 'hatred and repatriation' but instead to a spate of anthropologically curious Channel 4 documentaries.

These cultural shifts have profoundly altered the place of Jewish words in the English language and in the language of English Jews, in a way that hasn't happened since the Renaissance. Around that time there was a flurry of interest in Hebrew among English scholars which engendered an injection of Hebrew words into English. Hebrew was seen as a mythical, almost magical language. It was the key to esoteric Jewish teachings, for example Kabbalah, which were thought to contain within them secrets of Christian doctrine. Hebrew and Aramaic were also necessary to understand the distinctive logic of the Talmud, thought to be the chief bastion of Jewish resistance to Christianity. Among the Hebrew-based words that entered English around this time were *cabal* and *abracadabra*, expressions with a magical, esoteric flavour.

In the last decade or two, Yiddish and Hebrew terms have again begun to find their way into everyday British English (just as they trickled into American English half a century ago.) Today goyim wish you Happy Hanukah, laugh knowingly when you call yourself a *schlemiel* and decry the chutzpah of other motorists who double-park. When the Royal Institute of British Architects advertises its premises as the perfect place to hold your *simchah*, it's a sign either that the market for parties in posh surroundings is mostly Jewish, or that something intriguing is happening to the English language.

For British Jews, the changes have been no less pronounced. Thirty years ago, Jewish words in everyday currency didn't go much further than bar mitzvah, *bris* and bagel. Today things are much more confusing. You find yourself attending a *shiur* at the *shul*, your children go off to yeshivah and marry their *besherts*, at a *shivah* house people hardly wish each other 'long life' any more, but instead say '*hamakon y'hachem etchem im sha'ar avlei Tzion v'Yerushalayim*', which is altogether more of a mouthful. The multi-channelled return to Jewish life brings with it a sometimes bewildering influx of Jewish language.

There's nothing like language as a tool for creating insiders and outsiders. The flip side to the warm glow of belonging that comes with knowing the lingo is the alienation and resentment of ignorance. For Jews and non-Jews alike, when the flow of Jewish words outstrips our ability to absorb them, the characteristically British response is embarrassment and fear of having our ignorance exposed.

In the interests of transatlantic fairness, I should point out that today the unfamiliarity of US and UK Jews with Jewish words has converged. Of course, the US journey has taken a very different path to Jewish words' ignorance.

As Irving Howe recounts in his *World of Our Fathers*, the deracinating pressures on new Jewish immigrants at the turn of the twentieth century were far less intense.[3] Yiddish literature, journalism and theatre flourished in New York for half a century. Indeed, Howe shows that many of the immigrants learned Yiddish *after* arriving in the USA. The *mamaloshon* was the most accessible medium for finding a common culture with other Jews. Sixty years ago my great-grandmother, who emigrated from Germany to Britain, first visited New York and was scandalized to hear people speaking Yiddish on the buses without the slightest embarrassment.

This culture was celebrated by Leo Rosten's book, the *Joys of Yiddish*.[4] In many ways the 1960s in America corresponded to the last ten years in Britain as the time when Jews became mainstream in popular culture. Bellow and Malamud attained Great American Writer status, and Woody Allen began to play out the varieties of Jewish neurosis on screen. From these vantage-points, an unprecented volume of Jewish words entered American usage. But assimilation of US Jews has gathered speed since then. Today, my teenage cousin from Long Island can't tell *naches* from nachos. Mexican corn snacks play a larger role in his worldview than the pride of Jewish grandparents. The characteristic American response to

[3]   Irving Howe, *World of Our Fathers* (New York, 1976).
[4]   Leo Rosten, *The Joys of Yiddish* (London: Hamish Hamilton, 1967).

this is not embarrassment but a self-accepting shrug. Who today has the time to sample all the ingredients in the melting-pot?

So when in 2003 Simon Rocker of the *Jewish Chronicle* suggested writing a weekly column on Jewish words, I readily agreed, not just for the gratification of seeing my name in print, but because it seemed like a good way to reconnect readers with a missing part of their heritage.

At first I conceived the columns mainly as embarrassment therapy. I tried to imagine words that ordinary *Jewish Chronicle* readers might vaguely have heard of, but probably didn't entirely understand. My goal was to give a pithy 250-word gift-wrapped explanation of the meaning, etymology and contemporary usage of a word or phrase. No longer need my readers squirm when the rabbi declared in his sermon that it's time to *schrei gevalt* at some outrage, or not know whether to turn up in black hat or white tie if their religious relatives invited them to a *shevah berakhot.* Just by reaching for their *Jewish Chronicle* they could dispel their confusion, as well as the aura of smugness that so often clings to the initiated.

As the weeks went on, however, I realized that I was involved in something more ambitious. For to give a pen-portrait of a Jewish word, tracing its career in the language from origins to its current incarnations, is inevitably to give a snapshot of a slice of Jewish life. As Ludwig Wittgenstein put it, 'the meaning of a word is its use in the language'.[5] There are no mathematical formulae that can predict what a given word may or may not mean. One must look at the ways in which a word is used in actual forms of life to understand its meanings. Wittgenstein's insight seemed especially true of the words I was writing about. A biblical root could be subtly inflected in the Talmud, surface again as a term of art in medieval philosophy, go underground for generations, then pop up in the twentieth century as Zionist ideology or Yiddish slang. You can't predict such trajectories. All one can do is marvel at the ability of words to be projected into surprising yet natural new contexts and try to describe the process.

(This capacity for creative neologism makes describing words a useful tool for undercutting some of the divisions in the Jewish world. Jewish identity today is fragmented. There are those for whom it is a religion and nothing but; others are cultural Jews who profess themselves tone deaf to the music of spirituality, and there are still others for whom being Jewish is about food, ethnicity or nationality. Yet the same word can resonate in all of these different contexts. What connects the uses is that Jews have found ways to project them between the different spheres of their identity. The career of a word can bear witness to the fact of Jewish peoplehood, mysteriously binding across millennia, continents and ideologies.)

---

[5]   Ludwig Wittgenstein *Philosophical Investigations*, (Oxford, 1958) 20.

LET'S SCHMOOZE: JEWISH WORDS TODAY

As Wittgenstein also says, to speak a language is to understand a form of life. To explain when exactly you would call yourself a *schlemiel* rather than a *schlemazel*, or what you say at a *shiva*, or the Israeli milieu which gives the phrase *shalom haver* its particular poignancy goes far beyond dictionary definition. It's one thing to know that *ba'al teshuvah* (BT for short) is the proper word for your neighbour's son who goes off to yeshivah and comes back with *payos* flying and *tzitzit* hanging out. But to properly understand the word *teshuvah* (return) in this context involves renewing a spiritual worldview in which all creation is striving for closeness with the divine source of existence, which may be far more than the speaker bargained for. As Stanley Cavell of Harvard, one of the leading Wittgenstein interpreters suggests, we may have travelled so far from the forms of life in which certain words were used that we simply can't understand them.[6] (Cavell raises the posibility that 'God' might be such a word.)

So acquainting readers with unfamiliar Jewish words required drawing vignettes from the forms of life in which saying those things makes sense. It meant reviving contact with spiritual or cultural worlds that may have seemed dead or impossibly remote.

Wittgenstein and his followers called this procedure of bringing words back into attunement with their char-

---

[6] Stanley Cavell, *The Claim of Reason* (Oxford, 1979).

acteristic forms of life 'ordinary language philosophy'. Now, philosophy seems a thoroughly pretentious term for these skimpy accompaniments to *Jewish Chronicle* readers' Friday cornflakes or Shabbos afternoon *schluffs*. Nevertheless, the aspirations were related.

In turning the columns into a book, I've taken the opportunity to disaggregate the slices of Jewish life that the pieces describe in several ways. 'Jewish words' is itself a term invented for the purposes of my column and this book. I've included sections that highlight the contribution to 'Jewish words' of a range of linguistic sources, the Anglicized Hebrew of the King James Bible, Yiddish, modern Hebrew, Jewish religious life and the patois of the yeshivah. I've also divided the entries according to the circumstances in which readers might encounter them, whether in synagogue, on Jewish holidays or at life-cycle events. Finally, I've created sections by subject matter (e.g. food, magic and superstition), and names for the variegated subgroups of Jews.

This is not a book that is likely to satisfy purists and pedants (including the pedant in me). I am not an authority on most of the areas that I've written about. Often I cannot say for certain what the true etymology of a given word is. The Talmud says, 'a person should always train himself to say, "I don't know"' in cases where indeed he doesn't know. I have tried to follow its advice. Also, the fastidious reader will find that my transliterations are inconsistent. As a rule I have followed the system of the

Encyclopaedia Judaica. However, in cases where a word is rarely if ever written as the *EJ* says it should be, I have chosen the way in which the word usually appears in print.

Lateness is a proverbial Jewish trait. Times on wedding invitations are jokingly assumed to refer to 'Jewish Mean Time', which runs precisely 45 minutes behind GMT. (Perhaps this is because we think of ourselves as one big *mishpochah*; the family will understand.) So it's fairly typical that Jews should arrive at the multicultural party just when serious questions are being raised about the continuing viability of the whole enterprise. Pundits and politicians are wondering whether the fostering of immigrant cultures at the expense of integration has led to a dangerous isolation in parts of the Muslim community. In these debates, Britain's Jews are sometimes held up as a sterling example of how a minority group can thoroughly acculturate to British values while maintaining a strong and distinctive religious identity.

Now I'm all in favour of ethnic minorities being expected to conform to certain norms of civic behaviour, such as not blowing up people with whom you disagree. However, the trumpeting of the Anglo-Jewish example ignores the coercive aspect of the early twentieth-century Jewish experience, the reality of British anti-Semitism that made that coercion seem necessary to the community's leaders, and the high price in spiritual deracination that the Jews paid for their acceptance. It seems to me

INTRODUCTION

that there should be a way for ethnic communities to
assimilate norms of civic behaviour and political culture
without having to sacrifice so much of their heritage. In
the United States, which combines a strong immigrant
ethos with the demand for allegiance to an explicit
constititution, it's clearly possible to have it both ways. In
Britain we're still struggling to find the balance,
oscillating between nostalgia for a monolithic Englishness
and anything-goes cultural relativism.

I hope that as well as being fun and informative, this
collection will also show how one minority's presence has
enriched British and American language and life. My
deeper hope is that it may provoke readers to reconsider
the religious sources that continue to lend vitality to
Jewish language and life.

1

Words for Words

*This is the first column I wrote, in January 2003, in the
Jewish Chronicle. It can also be read as a second introduction
to this book.*

davar

Davar means 'word', and it also means 'thing'. This fact
reflects a deep facet of a Jewish worldview.

Words are the creative energy of the world. God spoke,
and through words brought the universe into being.

The kabbalists tell us that reality itself is forged from
combinations of the 22 Hebrew letters. There is a
mystical correspondence between a word and what it
refers to. We, too, create our world and the things of our
lives through words.

As Wittgenstein and others teach us, the words we use
are the way in which we each parcel out the amorphous
stuff of experience into manageable, useful objects and
concepts. How we do this tells us interesting things about
our culture. For instance, Eskimos have nearly 40

different words for snow, and English today has about 55 different slang expressions for throwing up. The Hebrew language has six words for 'soul'.

Our familiarity with, or distance from, Jewish words reflects a relationship to the things of Jewish life. To take a trivial example: how many people think that you *schlepp naches*? No, you *schepp naches*. *Schlepp* means 'carry', '*schepp*' means 'draw out' or 'derive'. (Look it up, or ask any great-grandparent.)

Thinking about Jewish words, whether familiar, strange, abused or misused, recovering the fullness and depth of their meaning, is a way of restoring and reinvigorating our connection to the life that they carry.

2

That's Funny: You Don't Look Jewish

These entries represent the verbal equivalent of the Sephardi Jews who came into Britain with Oliver Cromwell, respectable, centuries-old denizens of the English language that native speakers may encounter every day without paying any thought to their Jewish origins. Words designating things as English as the bunting and street parties of a royal anniversary or describing a particular clique of ministers that surrounded Charles II turn out to have Hebrew roots.

There are two main sources for these longstanding immigrants. The first is the intense flirtation with Hebrew among Renaissance scholars, which introduced a number of words of magical and esoteric flavour including cabal and abracadabra.

The second is the Bible. For centuries the Authorized Version was the most-read book in English. Hebrew words such as Jubilee that King James' translators deemed untranslatable became, ipso facto, *English.*

armageddon

Back in the 1980s, when all-out war between the superpowers was thought to be a real possibility, pundits often referred to the potential for 'nuclear armageddon'. Today the word is still in use, mainly among scary Christian sects who predict a final apocalyptic conflict.

The word 'armageddon' is taken from Christian eschatology (see Revelation 16.16) where it is the site of the ultimate battle foreseen between the forces of good and the forces of evil. The most widely accepted derivation of the name is that it is from the Hebrew, Har Megiddo, the mountain of Megiddo, referring to the 4,000-year-old settlement about 20 miles south-east of Haifa.

Megiddo was where King Josiah fell in battle against the Egyptians in the seventh century BCE. This is probably the origin of the association of Megiddo with war, which is also found in Zechariah 12.11.

An alternative etymology of armageddon is Har Migdo, 'God's fruitful mountain', which is taken to refer to Mount Zion. This would square with passages in the book of Joel (e.g. 2.1–3) which envisage this as the site of a great struggle between good and evil.

Either way, let's hope and pray that the world wakes up to the currently emerging nuclear threats before armageddon moves out of the lexicon of apocalyptic fanatics and into mainstream usage once again.

cabal

The now commonplace liberal-left claim that US foreign policy is run, to the detriment of the whole world, by a 'neo-con cabal' consisting of Richard Perle, Paul Wolfowitz and certain other shadowy (Jewish) figures has at least fostered a renewed public consciousness of this fascinating word (cabal, not neo-con).

'Cabal' entered the English language in the late sixteenth century to mean a secret intrigue, plot or conspiracy. This coinage coincided with the rising awareness of Jewish mystical teachings, the Kabbalah, in non-Jewish circles. (The word 'Kabbalah' derives from the word meaning 'receive', denoting the private, oral nature of its transmission from teacher to student.)

The Renaissance scholar Johannes Reuchlin had attempted to mine kabbalistic sources for proofs of the truth of Christianity. Even if most people didn't understand the details of Kabbalah, they knew it was something esoteric and secret, hence the word cabal.

The heyday of the word came in the mid-late seventeenth century. A committee of five ministers under Charles II was widely known as the Cabal. Fortuitously, their names – Clifford, Arlington, Buckingham, Ashley and Lauderdale – began with the letters C-A-B-A-L!

The fortunes of the neo-con cabal appear to be on the wane after the 2006 US congressional elections, but cabal is surely one of those anti-Semitic words ripe for reclaiming. Jews are successful, and hence influential, though not in any particularly sinister way. Join the cabal.

hallelujah

'Hallelujah' is a word best known from Harlem gospel churches (as in 'Hallelujah, praise the Lord') and from Handel's chorus. Many don't know that it's a Hebrew word that appears countless times in the book of Psalms.

Hallelujah is a combination of two words: *hallel*, meaning praise, and the shortened two-letter version of the name of God. For this reason some Jews won't pronounce the word except when reciting a prayer or a biblical verse, but will say *hallelukah* instead, rather than utter one of God's names in a profane context.

Hallel, the first part of the word, is also known to *shul*-goers as the celebratory singing of Psalms 113–18 on most Jewish holidays. Interestingly, we don't say *hallel* on Purim. The Talmud (Megillah 14a) suggests three possible explanations for this. The most challenging reason is that *hallel* simply doesn't apply to the Purim story. Why not? Because in the very first line of *hallel*, we say: 'Praise, you servants of God'. But at the end of the Purim story, though the Jews have been saved from death, they are still servants of Ahasuerus, subject to his anti-Semitic whims and caprices. Diaspora life continues as usual.

After the Purim story the Jews still cannot offer the wholehearted praise of servants of God, subject to no other master.

hosanna

'hosanna' is an English exclamation of praise or applause, and occurs in Jewish and Christian liturgy. Its origin is Hebrew. Hosanna is a contraction of *hoshiah-na*, which means 'Save [we] pray' (see Psalm 118.25).

On every day of Sukkot, during the morning service, the ceremony of Hoshanot takes place. The community encircles the *bimah* carrying the Torah scrolls and their four species (palm branch, willow, myrtle and citron) and recite a series of prayers repeating the refrain, *hoshana*, 'Save, please'.

This recreates a ritual that took place in the Temple. The Talmud describes how on each day of the festival, people would walk around the altar carrying their four species and singing *Hoshiah-na* (Sukkah 45a). The seventh day of Sukkot is called Hoshana Rabba (literally, the Big Hoshana), because on that day we encircle the *bimah* not once but seven times. The bundle of willow leaves that we carry on Hoshana Rabba is sometimes called *hoshanot* in honour of their role in the ceremony.

The idea behind the custom is that Sukkot is the time when the rainfall for the coming year is allocated (Talmud, Rosh Hashanah 16a). *Hoshanot* are a plea that we may be judged generously for rain, and for material blessings to be more widely understood in the coming year.

jubilee

A *jubilee* evokes images of bunting: Union Jacks and (more or less) spontaneous street parties celebrating some notable royal milestone.

It is actually derived from the Hebrew *yovel*. In the Torah, the *yovel* probably comes from an ancient term for the ram's horn sounded on Yom Kippur at the inauguration of each *yovel* year (Leviticus 25.9). (In the Talmud, Rabbi Akiva remarks that in Arabia, they call a ram *yubla*).

In the *yovel* year, all land was returned to its original owners. Any land acquisitions made during the previous 50 years were cancelled. Property reverted to the families who had held it when the Jewish people first entered the land of Israel. For 49 years, people were able to buy and sell land freely. In the 50th year, however, the inevitable inequalities thus generated were annulled, and everyone began again from the old baseline.

Today we do not observe the *yovel* and have lost count of when it occurs. However, it still represents a model of an ideal Jewish economic system, synthesizing egalitarianism with the free market. The Jubilee 2000 Third World debt relief campaign was inspired by the same idea of wiping out some of the accumulated disparities in power between rich and poor countries by freeing the poor from the permanent, self-perpetuating consequences of their mistakes or misfortunes.

mammon

'Mammon' has entered the English language as a synonym for filthy, corrupting riches, spawning such fearful conditions as mammonism (devotion to the pursuit of riches). This is mainly through the agency of the Christian Bible, where mammon gets a bad press (e.g., 'You cannot serve both God and mammon', Matthew 6.24). Mammon simply means money or wealth in the Hebrew of the time, but most English versions of the Gospels leave the Hebrew word untranslated, which lends to the love of money a Jewish sound.

In Mishnaic Hebrew, mammon doesn't have this negative sense. In origin it is a contraction of *mihamon*, where *mi* means from and *hamon* is mass or accumulation. *Dinei mammonot* are cases in monetary law, as opposed to *dinei nefashot*, capital cases. The Talmud (Bava Kamma 83b) wants us to know that the biblical phrase 'an eye for an eye' (Exodus 21.24) refers to mammon, monetary compensation rather than the actual putting out of an eye.

This neutral sense of mammon in the Jewish sources reflects a theological difference from Christianity. Mammon is not intrinsically good or bad: it's a matter of how you use it.

In Jewish law, holiness is achieved not by shunning the world of money but by sanctifying it through honest business dealings and generosity with what one has. If one wants to attain saintliness, the Talmud surprisingly tells us, study the laws of financial damages.

3

Magic and Superstition

Jewish magic and superstition covers a wide range of spells, amulets, incantations, astrologies, divining bowls, demonologies and assorted other folk beliefs. Some of it is rooted in Kabbalistic sources, much was imported from other cultures (especially the Babylonian in the Talmudic period and the Europe of the Middle Ages) and a good deal of it is sheer rubbish. Despite the efforts of Maimonides and other rationalist Jewish philosophers to purge Judaism of these elements, they have persisted in popular imagination, which is rarely governed by reason alone.

Indeed, the durability of these beliefs means that expressions for superstitions are among the longest surviving in assimilating Jews and so are disproportionately represented among words that have made it into mainstream English. Many are the grandparents today who will devoutly exclaim 'keneinahora' or 'poo, poo, poo' on hearing good news, without the faintest idea why, except that it's what their grandparents did.

atbash

Readers of Dan Brown's blockbusting thriller, *The Da Vinci Code*, will recall that the atbash cipher plays a crucial role in the verse clue that Jacques Saunière constructs as the key to the outer cryptex. (If you don't know what I'm talking about, don't worry and read on.)

Dan Brown's knowledge of Judaism is highly unreliable, but this happens to be one of the few things he got right.

The atbash cipher is a Hebrew code, which works by substituting the first letter of the alphabet for the last, the second for the second last, and so on. So *aleph* becomes *tav*, *bet* becomes *shin*, hence the name, atbash.

The Talmud discusses the method and gives a mnemonic for recalling the substitutions (Shabbat 104a).

According to the Talmud, there are atbash-coded words in the Bible itself. Jeremiah (25.26) says that, at last, the King of Sheshach will be forced to drink from the cup of divine wrath.

Sheshach is not a town of which the Talmud (Megillah 6a) has heard, and it states that Sheshach is, in fact, Bavel, or Babylon. Rashi explains that this is based on atbash substitution. (Take a pen and paper and try it: it works.)

If Jeremiah encodes the name Bavel in this prophecy against the city, it may be because the book was written under Babylonian rule.

chamsa

The *chamsa*, a hand-shaped good-luck amulet, is the cool souvenir to bring back from Israel these days. *Chamsas* are everywhere, from the rear-view mirrors of taxi drivers, to the trendiest jewellery shops. Though more common among Sephardi Jews, they are crossing over to the Ashkenazi community too.

The word *chamsa* derives from the Semitic root meaning 'five', as in five fingers. It is a remarkably ancient and ecumenical sign, representing the protective hand of God. Sometimes *chamsas* also have a single eye embedded in the middle, symbolizing God's loving oversight.

Chamsas have long been a good-luck symbol for Jews, Christians and Muslims living around the Mediterranean. The different religions have called it the eye of Miriam, the eye of Mary and the eye of Fatima, respectively. Some scholars claim that the symbol is older than all of them, and attribute it to ancient Canaanite, Philistine and Phoenician cults, who used to make a gesture signifying the hand of Baal over their heads to protect themselves from the evil eye.

Interestingly, some Jewish *chamsas* have six fingers. This may well reflect an unease at the idolatrous possibilities in a symbol which is meant somehow to represent a body-part of God. (Since Maimonides, the overwhelming majority view in Jewish theology has been that God does not have a body.) Depicting a hand that is not a real hand avoids the problem of literal representation.

kenainahora

When I was small, elderly relatives used to invoke the word *keneinahora* to qualify certain cheerful or optimistic statements, e.g. 'She's a clever girl, *keneinahora*', or 'Spurs won again on Shabbos, *keneinahora*'.

It was a long time until I realized that *keneinahora* actually meant something. It is in fact a Yiddishized running together of *kein ayin hara*. *Kein* means no or without in German and Yiddish, whilst *ayin hara* refers to the evil eye in Hebrew.

The evil eye is an ancient Jewish superstition. Good fortune should not be celebrated too loudly and ostentatiously, lest it draw the attention of the evil eye – a spiritual force that would snatch away our blessings.

To this day, there are widespread Jewish traditions whose rationale is to avoid the evil eye, such as the practice of not calling up members of one family to the Torah consecutively, or of people whose parents are both living leaving the synagogue during Yizkor, the memorial prayer for the dead.

Some ridicule such customs as archaic and irrational. In their defence, one can say that they have a moral dimension. Not flaunting one's good fortune in other people's faces is admirable – even if the result is to reinforce a superstition.

Satan

It's a long way from the first appearance of the root of the word Satan in the Torah, to the men (and it does seem to be mainly men) with long hair in leather and chains on motorbikes. The angel who appears to Balaam comes to him *l'satan*, meaning to obstruct or oppose him on his journey. This is the particular task for which the angel was sent. There's no indication that it's the angel's permanent job.

In most biblical instances of the word Satan, it means a human adversary (e.g. 1 Samuel 29.4). In 1 Chronicles 21.1, Satan is an angel who tempts David to count the people; and most famously in Job, Satan becomes Job's accuser in heaven.

In the Mishnah and Gemara, there are scattered references to Satan as the voice of temptation to sin. The Talmud Yoma 20a notes that the *gematria* (numerical equivalent) of Hasatan, 'the Satan', is 364 and infers from this that on one day a year, Yom Kippur, Satan has no power to seduce human beings. In Talmud Berachot 9a we meet the well-known phrase, 'to open your mouth to Satan', meaning to tempt fate.

Jewish sources don't contain the image of Satan as anti-Christ, the author and ultimate personification of evil, that has entered the popular imagination through the Gospels and Milton.

shedim

Shedim are demons. People in the circles I move in don't really believe in them except as figures of speech. You might say 'the *shedim* came and made my chicken soup boil over'. (Hasidic sources say *shedim* are particularly intent on spoiling one's preparations in the last moments before Shabbat. I can well believe it.)

In the Bible, *shedim* means foreign gods (see Deuteronomy 32.17). The word is related to the Akkadian *sedu*, meaning demon. It's tempting to speculate whether there's any connection with the Old English 'shade', meaning spirit, which derives from the Greek *skotos*, meaning darkness. (I supect there isn't, but lack the learning to say for sure.)

In the past, many Jews did believe in *shedim*. The Babylonian Talmud refers to them, probably under the influence of the local culture which knew of a profusion of demons. Rabbi Yochanan Ben Zakkai mastered every important branch of knowledge, and in addition understood the speech of *shedim* (Sukkah 28a).

Shedim live in deserts, dirty places or ruins. They are particularly fond of privies. One needs to watch out for them especially around uncovered food or water. This suggests that *shedim* may have been an explanation for the observed health risks accompanying these things.

Belief in *shedim* persisted well into the Middle Ages. The great rationalist philosopher Maimonides had no truck with them and began the process of booting *shedim* out of Judaism once and for all.

4

Food

Food is a major marker of ethnicity. Nostalgia for the smells and tastes of moma or bubba's kitchen can persist long after religious practice has been shed. So not surprisingly, schmaltz *and* kishkes, *etc. have taken their place in English alongside ravioli, enchiladas and chop suey.*

The fierce debate about the proper pronunciation of bagel *(whether* bagel *rhymes with 'Hegel', or with 'my girl') bears witness to the commonness of the word. So too, the remarkable prevalence today of the phrase, 'What am I, chopped liver?' (i.e. don't I count for anything?) suggests that Shabbat appetizer's familiarity.*

Indeed, food is popularly believed to play a larger role in Jewish culture than in Italian, Mexican or Chinese cultures. The chicken soup ladle-wielding Jewish mother is a cliché of stand-up comedy. There may also be some truth in it. Celebrations of Jewish holidays (apart from fast days) invariably involve food. The line 'they tried to kill us, God saved us, let's eat', is a gross oversimplification of the Jewish calendar, but at least approximates to the observance of a

29

couple of the holidays. No doubt others have also psychologized about food being a surrogate for love in a disintegrating ethnic community.

challah

Challah, the plaited white loaf that we eat at Shabbat meals, is among the best-known Jewish religious objects. Last time I was in New York, I passed a café on Broadway advertising bacon and eggs with challah rolls. As usual the USA is far ahead of us in catapulting cultural Judaism, shorn of its religious roots, into the mainstream.

In the Bible, challah is the portion of bread that is set aside and given to the priests to eat (Numbers 15.19–20). The *mitzvah* of separating challah applies to the five grains, wheat, barley, spelt, oats and rye. The rabbis calculate that more than 1.75 kg of dough baked at one time must have challah taken from it.

According to the Torah, the *mitzvah* of challah is relevant only in the Land of Israel. However, the rabbis instituted it outside Israel as well, so that the *mitzvah* should not be forgotten. Nowadays, the custom when baking a sufficiently large amount of bread is to break off a small piece of dough the size of an olive and burn it.

According to the *Encyclopaedia Judaica*, one derivation is from the Hebrew root *challal*, meaning 'hollow', suggesting a rounded loaf; another possibility is that it comes from the Akkadian *ellu*, meaning 'pure', referring to the bread's sacred use.

The medieval compendium, Sefer Hamitzvot, says that the reason for challah, aside from the obvious one of supporting the priests, is that since our lives depend on bread, God gave us a *mitzvah* to fulfil whenever we bake, so that our bread may be blessed continuously.

cholent

A *cholent* is a stew of beans, barley, potatoes, onions and meat, which many Jews eat for lunch on Shabbat. *Kishkes* (stuffed intestines) and hard-boiled eggs are also optional ingredients, as is just about anything else that you feel like throwing in.

The rationale for *cholent* is to have the pleasure of eating hot food on Shabbat. Although the *halakhah* does not allow cooking on Shabbat, it permits you to keep warm food which was already cooked before sunset on Friday. *Cholent* is one of the rare foods which is actually enhanced by simmering for 20 hours on a hotplate, making it an ideal Shabbat lunch entrée.

Although the etymology of *cholent* is as murky as the stuff itself, the most likely explanation is that it is a corruption of the medieval French, *chaud-lent*, meaning 'hot-slow', alluding to the mode of its cooking.

One of the most remarkable paeans to the dish was penned by Rabbi Zerachya Halevi, the twelfth-century Talmudic commentator. He opines that if someone doesn't eat *cholent* on Shabbat, there is reason to suspect that he may be a heretic.

This ostensibly rather extreme view is directed at the Karaite heresy, which affirmed only the literal meaning of the biblical text and rejected rabbinic interpretation. While the rabbis permitted keeping warm food cooked before Shabbat, a person who denied rabbinic authority would deny himself this pleasure.

hamantashen

As a child I was told that *hamantashen*, the word for the triangular cakes we eat on Purim, means Haman's pockets in Yiddish. This always seemed highly improbable. Why would we make fun of the villain of the Megillah by eating representations of his pockets, rather than, say, some other part of his dress or anatomy?

In fact, this probably isn't the derivation at all. *Hamantashen* were originally *muntaschen*, pockets of poppy seeds, the traditional filling. Today, most *hamantashen* are chocolate (at least in our house). At a certain point they were renamed after Ahasuerus's evil vizier.

In Hebrew, *hamantashen* are known as *oznei Haman*, Haman's ears, which some may find distasteful although it makes more sense than the Yiddish, both geometrically and poetically. Eating *oznei Haman* is of a piece with the mocking dressing-up, noise-making and lampoonery of Purim in general. It's fashionable to find this troublingly triumphalistic. I think it very healthy.

To share a world with people who declare unequivocally their intention to destroy you is undoubtedly stressful, then and now. The fear of such threats can induce paralysis or denial. Laughing occasionally at those who make them is a way of continuing to live with clear-sightedness and optimism in such a world.

kishke

Kishke is a great Ashkenazi delicacy. You can eat it on its own, or use it to beef up the cholent for Shabbat. It's one of those items of Jewish cuisine, like jellied calf's foot (*pcha*), the origins of which you're probably better off not knowing.

For those who need to know the truth, *kishke* is cow's intestine stuffed with mincemeat, rice, vegetables and flour.

Kishke is Yiddish, but other Eastern European languages have a similar word for intestines: *kiszka* in Polish and *kishka* in Ukrainian or Russian.

Kishke has entered mainstream American English as a synonym for guts, bearing the connotation of emotional intensity that is popularly associated with Yiddish culture. 'A funny feeling about it in my *kishkes*', means that I have an irrational, but frequently reliable intuition.

'Oy, that story, it gets me right here in the *kishkes*' – usually accompanied by a dramatic slap of the belly – means that I have a powerful emotional response to the narrative.

In Israel today, *kishke* along with *pcha*, *knishes* (potato dumplings) and other Eastern European specialities, is almost unobtainable. This is in a country where hummus and felafel, the staples of North African and Middle Eastern cuisine, are available on every street corner.

Much has been said about the continuing cultural dominance of the Ashkenazim over the Sephardim. In culinary matters, however, the people have clearly made their choice.

lehem

Lehem, the Hebrew word for bread, is familiar to most of us from the *hamotzi* blessing said at Shabbat dinners, weddings and bar mitzvahs and, by observant Jews, whenever they eat bread.

The word itself appears to be a very ancient one referring to the most primal, basic foodstuff. In the Bible, it is often used metonymically to refer not just to bread, but to all food, the first instance being 'by the sweat of your brow you shall eat bread' (Genesis 3.19). Halakhically, this idea is expressed by the rule that the blessing for bread covers all the different types of food eaten at the same meal. Today, the Arabic word for meat is *lahme*, which suggests the same root meaning 'basic food', applied in a different culture to a different foodstuff.

Intriguingly, the word *lehem* is embedded in the word *milhamah*, which means 'war'. Leo Orenstein of Stanmore pointed out to me that Rabbi Samson Raphael Hirsch (1808–88) makes a connection between the two words in his Torah commentary. Hirsch asserts that *lehem* is the root of *milhamah* because wars are usually rooted in conflicts over the raw materials necessary for subsistence. War in the ancient world apparently involved one group of people consuming another, with all of its land, flocks, servants, women, etc. Hirsch may also have been influenced in this interpretation by the Marxist ideas current in his time. Today, human beings have discovered more sophisticated reasons for fighting one another.

seudah

Seudah means a meal, especially a festive one. There is a *mitzvah* to eat three *seudot* on Shabbat (Talmud Shabbat 118b), two on Yomtov and to make a *seudat mitzvah*, a feast around joyful religious acts such as weddings, bar mitzvahs, circumcisions, etc. Lubavitch Hasidim have a tradition to hold a *seudat Moshiach* on the day after Pesach, anticipating the arrival of the Messiah.

There's a joke going around that the basic structure of most Jewish holidays is 'they tried to kill us, we won, let's eat'. This has a grain of truth to it. As everyone knows, food plays a big part in Judaism. However, the crassness of the description comes from a pornography-of-food TV cooking-show culture that can't conceive of eating as a spiritual act.

How does one raise up the physiological act of eating? One may turn it into an aesthetic experience graced by good taste, refinement, culinary expertise and beautiful table settings – the cooking-show model. This, Rabbi

Joseph Soloveitchik argues, is not enough to redeem the act of eating. What transforms it into a religious act is infusing it with *hesed*, generosity and kindness.

The word *seudah* itself drives from the verb *sa'ad*, meaning to sustain, or support (Genesis 18.5; Psalm 104.5). By inviting guests, bringing in the poor and the lonely, and sharing wisdom as well as food, one turns a meal into a *seudah* and binds a group of individuals feeding into a community.

ta'am

Monty Python's classic film, *The Meaning of Life*, translates into Hebrew as *ta'am hachayim*. An American newspaper recently (and nonsensically) translated an Israeli politician saying that 'there is no *ta'am* [sense] in the question' as saying 'the matter has no taste'.

These examples illustrate the expanded sense of the word *ta'am*, beyond the meanings of the English word 'taste', which is its dictionary translation. *Ta'am* does indeed mean taste, as in the sensory faculty that is located in the mouth, and is also the word used in the Hebrew equivalent of the expression 'there's no accounting for taste', denoting one's general likes and dislikes.

However, *ta'am* also means something like discernment, or common-sense reasoning. Medieval Jewish philosophy expanded and popularized the area of study known as *ta'amei hamitzvot*, usually translated as reasons for the commandments.

Maimonides writes that it is possible to find reasons for the Torah's commandments; they should not be taken as senseless, irrational decrees (Guide for the Perplexed 3.26). The contemporary thinker Rabbi Yeshayahu Kronman points out that using the word *ta'am*, rather than, say, *sibah*, for reason, suggests that the reasons we find are subjective, intuitive ones that make sense to us, rather than the divinely intended rationale behind the commandments.

Psalm 119.65 expresses a similar idea. 'Teach me good reason [*ta'am*] and knowledge, for I have believed in Your commandments.' Understanding of the commandments flows best from commitment to them rather than from standing in judgement over them.

5

The Jewish Year

Most Jews have some connection to the holidays and the family celebrations that go with them. Goyim too have often heard of them through schoolmates and work colleagues. When I went to school in the 1970s and 1980s, a request to take the day off for Yom Kippur was greeted with faint, weary recognition. An appeal the following week to have time off for Sukkot would be met by downright disbelief, as if I'd conjured the holiday out of my imagination. (They tell me that things are better now.)

The Jewish year is the DNA of Judaism. Its endlessly replicated patterns contain within them the messages that Jews have been carrying for the past 3,000 years. Rosh Hashanah expresses the constant possibility of renewal. Yom Kippur is the aspiration to be better people next year than last. Pesach is about the unquenchable belief in freedom for ourselves, the Jewish nation and all humanity. Shavuot marks our receiving the spiritual task of Torah. Sukkot stands for thankfulness for what we have as we live under divine protection. Hanukah and Purim celebrate the extraordinary survival of the Jewish people against impossible odds.

Living and understanding the Jewish holidays is an essential way of accessing the spiritual path of Judaism. In this section I have not attempted to describe the holy days and festivals in detail (they are reasonably well known, and certainly to Jews); rather I have endeavoured to explain a few of the concepts, artefacts and expressions that are an integral part of their celebration.

afikomen

The *afikomen* is the piece of the middle matzah at the Pesach Seder which ends up being pulverized under the carpet, in the DVD player, or in whatever other brilliant hiding-place Dad thought of this year.

The etymology of *afikomen* is interesting. It comes from Greek meaning literally 'around (*epi-*) the meal.' Jastrow's Talmudic Dictionary quotes Plutarch using the Latin version, *commessatum*, to mean 'to the after-dinner entertainment.' On this reading, the enigmatic statement of the *Mishnah*, 'Ein maftirin achar ha-Pesach Afikomen' (Pesachim, 10.8) means 'After the Seder meal is finished, one shouldn't finish off by saying "Let's go to the after-dinner entertainment"'. The after-dinner entertainment that evening is to carry on talking about the Exodus from Egypt late into the night.

According to a variant of this view, *afikomen* was a Greek practice of going from house to house after dinner for a snack. The rabbis wanted to prevent this happening on Seder night, so that people would celebrate the whole occasion with the same family group. The *afikomen matzah* which is the last food we taste at the meal is instead of the *afikomen* practice of roaming the streets after dinner.

din

Din means judgement. Rosh Hashanah is also known as Yom Hadin, the Day of Judgement. On Rosh Hashanah the whole world is judged (Mishnah Rosh Hashanah, 1.2). This accounts for the ambivalent character of the day. It's a *yomtov*. We wear white and eat, drink and rejoice, but we don't say *hallel*; we hope and pray that God's judgement will be tempered by love, yet at a time of judgement our joy is restrained.

Judgement is something we're suspicious of these days. 'Non-judgementalism has been universally accepted as the highest, indeed the only virtue', writes social commentator Theodore Dalrymple. We understand that actions have precipitating causes. We're more sophisticated than to judge others and we expect God to be also.

Yet Rosh Hashanah makes us confront our mortality, and so our responsibility to make our lives count. We have limited time and only we are accountable for how we spend it, for good or ill, to help or harm.

Din, writes the contemporary teacher Rabbi Matis

Weinberg, means not only judgement but consequence. Our choices have outcomes that may hurt ourselves or others. *Din*, searching, honest and critical judgement, is the way through which we may recognize and repair unhealthy or destructive patterns of life and start to restore ourselves to spiritual health.

dreidl

Dreidl is a children's game, played with a spinning-top that is universally associated with Hanukah. A popular legend ascribes its origin to the Jewish children at the time of the Hasmonean revolt. The evil Antiochus forbade the Jews to study Torah, so to evade the decree, Jewish children hid and studied in caves. When discovered, they would conceal their books, whip out their *dreidls* and pretend to be playing a harmless game.

This is a pretty story, consistent with the timeless meaning of Hanukah, but with no basis in historical fact. It appears that *dreidl* was a medieval German gambling game. (The word itself comes from the German, *trudeln*, meaning to spin, or possibly *drehen*, to rotate.)

In the original version, the four sides of the top were marked with the letters n, g, h and s, standing for *nichts* (nothing), *ganz* (take all), *halb* (take half) and *stell ein* (put into the kitty). In Yiddish/Hebrew, these letters became *nun, heh, gimmel, shin*. This was taken to stand for *ness gadol hayah sham*, meaning, 'a great miracle happened there', i.e., in the Land of Israel.

Consequently, *dreidls* in Israel replace the letter *shin* with *peh*, to make the phrase '*ness gadol hayah poh*', or, 'a great miracle happened here'.

Dreidl is thus a beautiful example of how Judaism can absorb an outside practice and imbue it with Jewish significance.

eruv

The word *eruv* has been very much in the news lately. This slender border is set to transform life for many of London's Orthodox Jews, especially women. National newspapers have run learned halakhic analyses of the boundary within which Jews in Barnet can now carry or push some otherwise prohibited items on Shabbat.

While much has been written on the legal issues of the *eruv*, less has been said about the word itself. The root of *eruv* means to 'mix,' or 'mingle together.'

The simplest kind of *eruv*, for the purposes of carrying, was organized by adjacent householders agreeing to mix together their individual holdings to create one large, shared private domain. Within this area, all of the participants could carry on Shabbat just as they could within their own homes. (This is not an explanation for how the modern *eruv* works.)

Erev, (evening) and *ma'ariv* (evening prayer) are close relatives. Evening is the time when day and night mingle and interpenetrate. *Arev*, meaning 'guarantor', also shares the same root. (In Israel, *arevim* are required for many private rental contracts. They are the people who pay if the tenants trash the place.)

An *arev* is someone whose status and responsibilities are inseparably mixed up with the person he is guaranteeing. Judah declares to Jacob that he will be *arev* for his brother Benjamin when they go to Egypt: he makes himself personally responsible for Benjamin's fate.

The Talmud states: 'All Jews are *arevim*, guarantors for one another.' In context, this principle explains how we can do certain *mitvzot* on each other's behalf. More generally, it speaks of our indissoluble connections with other Jews, our obligation to support one another when in trouble, and our profound, often inexplicable, sense of being mixed up in the destiny of Jews everywhere.

Haggadah

Haggadah is the telling of the story of going out of Egypt on Seder night, and Haggadah the name of the book from which we tell the story.

Transmitting the tale of that formative event in Jewish history is crucial to passing on Judaism to our children. The Torah even suggests that the Exodus happened so that we would tell the story to the coming generations (Exodus 10.2).

The root of *haggadah* is *haggad*, which means, 'to draw [a line]'. The transitive version *higid* then comes to mean 'to show, announce, demonstrate or tell'.

The etymology tells us that *haggadah* is accomplished not

just through words, but by anything that enacts the story. According to the nineteenth-century commentator Malbim, the Haggadah is so called because it is not just words, but a multi-media dramatization of going out of Egypt.

The leaning, eating matzah and bitter herbs, the symbolic props on the Seder plate, the custom in some families to stagger around the table with heavy sacks, and then throw them away, are all meant as an invitation to enact the story in the most vivid and engaging way possible.

Kinot

Kinot are the elegiac poems and lamentations that we say in the synagogue on Tisha b'Av. They are usually recited while sitting on the floor or on low stools as a sign of mourning for the destruction of the Temple and the subsequent tragedies in Jewish history which are connected to Tisha b'Av.

Kinot that were composed in the wake of these events have been continuously added to the liturgy. As well as laments over the Temple, there are also *kinot* inspired by the Crusades, the York Massacre of 1190, the expulsion of the Jews from England in 1290, the Spanish expulsion and the Shoah.

Kinah means to wail, cry or lament. It is first used in the Bible when David mourns the death of Saul and Jonathan with the words, 'How are the mighty fallen' (2 Samuel 1.19).

In Jeremiah (9.16) we read of the *m'konnenot*, professional mourners whose job was to keen and wail at funerals to create an appropriate atmosphere. (*M'konnenot* apparently also existed in other cultures at the time.)

The mourning of Tisha b'Av is not meant as an occasion to wallow in grief, but rather to sharpen our yearning for the Temple and for a rebuilt and peaceful Jerusalem. The Talmud says that one who shares in the grief of Jerusalem will deserve to see its comforting.

lehem oni

Lehem oni is the first name for matzah that we encounter on Seder night, when we declare '*Ha lahma anya*', 'This is the bread of poverty', and invite the needy to share our meal.

Rabbi Joseph Soloveitchik (1903–93) wrote that this is a pledge of solidarity among the Jewish people. By sharing in the bread of suffering, we affirm our brotherhood with all in need, whether the hungry needing food, or the lonely craving company.

Many have remarked on the paradox, that matzah is described as both *lehem oni*, the poor, rough bread, that our ancestors were fed as slaves in Egypt (because it's a cheap way to fill your stomach, according to one commentator), and as the bread of freedom which they ate on their way out.

The Maharal of Prague (1525–1609) suggested a famous resolution. When we are encumbered by superfluities, symbolized by the puffiness of bread, it is difficult to make a break from oppressive conditions. The simplicity that matzah denotes enables freedom.

The Talmud (Pesachim 36a) punningly construes *lehem oni* as 'bread upon which we answer (*onim*) many things'. This is not the literal meaning of *lehem oni*, but it captures a vital feature of the matzah. It is meant to provoke us to conversation, to questions stimulated by its strangeness, and multiple answers that draw us into the timeless story of the exodus from Egypt, formative for Jewish identity to this day.

Mah nishtanah

Mah nishtanah, meaning 'What is made different?' is a phrase known to anyone who's been to the first ten minutes of a Seder night.

It has even entered common usage as an ironic way of questioning unusual behaviour; to someone who's habitually late but for once turns up on time, you might ask '*Mah nishtanah...?*'

Mah nishtanah is the opening of the Four Questions (five if you count *Mah nishtanah* itself) traditionally asked by the youngest child present at the Seder. The questions point out four obvious ways in which 'this night is different from all other nights'. If there are no children, the adults ask one another. If you are alone, you should ask yourself (Talmud Pesachim 116a).

Provoking questions is essential to the Seder. In fact,

the text of *Mah nishtanah* is a sort of fallback plan that's necessary only if no one asks.

We are supposed to do something different, or surprising, on Seder night to get the children to ask in spontaneous amazement and without the need for a script. Some rabbis removed the table before dinner or gave special treats to the kids to stimulate wonder and engender new questions (Pesachim 115b). A good question shakes us out of fixed routines of thought and opens us up to genuine learning.

When we really feel how different this night is, we are ready to hear the Haggadah's answer to why it is that God intervened to save our ancestors from the crushing routine of slavery, and introduced different principles of freedom and human dignity to be motive forces of history.

menorah/hanukiah

The nine-branched candlestick on which we light ascending numbers of candles over the eight days of Hanukah is commonly known as a *menorah* and occasionally as a *hanukiah*. *Menorah* means 'light-source', deriving from the word *or* (light). *Hanukiah* implies something that we use specifically for Hanukah.

Hanukah, in turn, comes from the word *l'hanech*, meaning 'to dedicate', since Hanukah celebrates the rededication of the Temple. (*Hinuch*, meaning, 'education', derives from the same root; in Hebrew, education is dedication of oneself or a child to a way of life.)

The words are not interchangeable. In fact, the Hanukah candelabra is not a *menorah*, but a *hanukiah*. There are at least two important differences between them. Firstly, the *menorah*, whose details and dimensions are described in Exodus 25.31–40, had seven branches. The *hanukiah* has nine so that we can light a lamp for each of the eight nights, plus one more for the *shammes*.

Second, and more fundamentally, the *menorah* refers only to the candlestick which was used in the sanctuary and later in the Temple in Jerusalem.

Jews may not build a house on the design of the Temple, nor construct replicas of the Temple's accessories for some other use. For this reason we may not make a seven-branched candlestick (Talmud, Avodah Zara, 43a). To do so compromises the irreplaceable uniqueness of the Temple and its service.

muktzeh

Muktzeh means 'set aside' or 'stored away', from the root *katzeh*, which means 'edge'.

It's most commonly used to refer to the halakhic category of objects which may not be moved on Shabbat or Yomtov.

In our house on Shabbat, you may hear Ayala, who is 3, admonishing Moshe, aged 1, when the latter removes the phone from its cradle, 'No, Moshe, that's *muktzeh*'.

Objects may be *muktzeh* for a range of reasons: because their customary use is for some non-Shabbat-friendly purpose, like a phone; or because they have been set aside for use in a *mitzvah*, such as fruit hung up to decorate a *sukkah* during Sukkot (so you can't pick it to eat); or because they have no obvious Shabbat use, such as coins.

The concept of *muktzeh* plays a special role in creating the atmosphere of Shabbat. Objects which have only workday uses and associations are off-limits. Fiddling and fidgeting with things that set off a train of weekday worries is forbidden.

The way we relate to physical objects on Shabbat is transformed. This helps create and safeguard the oasis of Shabbat space in which we can be at peace.

Omer

The Omer is the 49-day period which we count from Pesach to Shavuot. It has multiple meanings and associations.

The word *omer* means 'sheaf' or 'bundle'. In the Torah (Leviticus 23.10), it refers to the sheaf of barley which was brought to the Temple from the first of the new crop on the second day of Pesach. It symbolizes renewal and thanks.

The Torah then tells us to count 49 days until we bring another grain offering on Shavuot, this time two finished loaves of bread. This latter offering symbolizes fullness and completion of the counting process.

Since the rabbinic period, the Omer has become a

semi-sad season. At least until the 33rd day, the *halakhah* is that we don't get married, have haircuts or listen to live music. This is in remembrance of the students of Rabbi Akiva who died from a plague during this time because, the Talmud tells us, they didn't treat one another with respect.

For the kabbalists, the Omer is a period of spiritual purification. There is a long road to travel from the Jews' sudden and hasty exodus from the slavery and idolatry of Egypt to arriving at the foot of Mount Sinai and being ready to make a covenant with God on the Torah.

In the mystical view, each of the 49 days of the Omer is a step on this journey and an opportunity to mend a different aspect of the human personality in preparation for receiving the Torah anew on Shavuot.

oneg Shabbat

In the student and youth movement worlds, an *oneg Shabbat* (or *oneg* for short) is a post-dinner programme on Friday night, usually involving crisps, marshmallows, singing and cheap alcohol.

In fact, *oneg Shabbat* is a halakhic term for the sheer physical enjoyment we should take in Shabbat. (*Oneg* literally means pleasure or delight.) Isaiah 58 says: 'You shall call the Shabbat a delight [*oneg*] and the holy thing of God shall be honoured'.

How is this sublime requirement of *oneg* to be fulfilled, the Talmud wonders. Rabbi Yehudah answers, 'through

eating spinach, large fish and heads of garlic'. Rav Pappa
says that it may be fulfilled even with something small like
little fish fried in oil and flour (Talmud Shabbat 118b).
It's typical of the *halakhah* to seek such mundane physical
expression for lofty values.

Today, we fulfil *oneg Shabbat* by eating three meals and
buying and preparing the best food and drink we can
afford. Sexual intimacy (for a married couple) is also a
part of *oneg Shabbat* (Maimonides, Laws of Shabbat
30.14).

The Talmud promises lavish spiritual rewards to those
who make Shabbat an *oneg*, a delight. Throughout the ups
and downs of our history, Jews have made sacrifices in
order to make Shabbat special, creating a weekly oasis of
joy and delight.

Shabbat

Shabbat is the day of rest which Jews celebrate every
week. The word itself has multiple, connected meanings.
Lashevet means to sit. Shabbat means to cease, as God
did on the seventh day in the creation story. *L'hashbit* is
the word the Torah uses for removing *hametz* before
Pesach.

The combination of sitting and ceasing gives the word,
'Shabbat' the sense of resting. Shabbat is a day of
relaxation and renewal attained through stopping our
weekday actions and routines. By ceasing creative or
transformative doing, (defined by the Torah under 39

categories of *melakha*) we clear space to simply be: with ourselves, our families and friends, and with God.

The Torah gives two reasons for Shabbat: a commemoration of creation, and a reminder of our being slaves in Egypt. The revolutionary social implications of Shabbat have often been noted. Slaves don't have a day off. Mandating a society-wide weekly holiday confers at least a minimum of freedom and dignity on all. Michael Walzer points out that Shabbat is far more egalitarian than a vacation, in that it cannot be bought. He also shows that the the etymology of vacation is quite different. In Rome, days on which there were no religious festivals were called *Dies vacantes*, 'empty days'. Shabbat, on the other hand, is full: of obligations and also of celebrations.

Shanah Tovah

There is some confusion about what one should wish people on Yom Kippur. '*Chag Sameach*' (happy festival), or '*Mo'adim l'simchah*' (occasions for joy), are not quite right. Yom Kippur has an aspect of *simchah*, joy, in that it is a time of forgiveness, but joy is restrained by awe at the Day of Judgement.

'Good Yomtov' is always a safe bet, and '*Gmar hatimah tovah*', 'May you be sealed for good (in the coming year)', is quite correct.

'*Shanah Tovah*', (A good year, is also appropriate. The Hebrew word *shanah* has two associations that appear contradictory. On the one hand, it means to repeat, or to do a second time (related to *sheni*, the number two.) The Jewish year is a cycle of sacred times that is repeated endlessly. On the other hand *l'shanot* means to change, modify or distinguish. The repetition provides an annual chance for change.

Yom Kippur is an opportunity to decide that next year will be different from last year. By resolving to do things differently and sincerely regretting the past, we can, with God's help, break free of the endless chain of consequences that our mistakes set in motion and make the year's repetition a chance for transformation.

shofar

Shofar is the ram's horn that we sound each morning during the month of Ellul, on Rosh Hashanah, (unless it falls on Shabbat) and at the close of Yom Kippur.

The word 'shofar' comes from a root meaning rounded which describes the shape of the shofar. (A *sh'foforet* is a tube or egg-shell.) This shape was not uncontroversial. The Talmud (Rosh Hashanah 26b) cites an argument about whether the Shofar for Rosh Hashanah should preferably be bent to symbolize a bowed and contrite posture on the Day of Judgement, or straight to indicate our upwards yearning.

Related to this sense of roundedness, *shafar* means smooth, pleasing or cheerful, and the verb *shiper* means to cleanse, conciliate or harmonize. These cognate meanings allow for some creative midrashic puns. For example, in the month of Tishrei, when the shofar is sounded, we must *shapru* (cleanse or harmonize) our deeds. (Vayikra Rabba, 29.)

The shofar blasts have accumulated many symbolic meanings, though none more famous or disturbing than Maimonides' suggestion (Hilkhot Teshuva, 3.4.) that it is a call to self-awareness: 'Wake up, sleepers ... get up, slumberers ... examine your actions, repent, and remember your Creator ... these are the people who forget the Truth in the toils of time, and strive for years after vanity and emptiness that cannot help or save them ...'

simchat beit hashoevah

If you walk through Meah Shearim any night during Hol Hamoed (the intermediate days) of Sukkot, you'll hear the sound of shlock-rock music booming from *simchaot beit hashoevah* in *yeshivot* and Hasidic courts in every street and courtyard.

A *simchat beit hashoevah* is a party for Sukkot. The source for these celebrations is the rejoicing at the water-drawing ceremony which took place in the Temple. The Talmud (Sukkah, Chapter 5) gives a long and picturesque account of the revelries which took place there. A torch-lit procession led to the House of Water-drawing. Noted rabbis performed their particular songs and dances. One was renowned for being able to do a handstand on his thumbs. The Talmud says that someone who never saw the *simchat beit hashoevah* never saw real rejoicing in his life.

There are clues in the Talmud to the nature of the intense joy which characterized the *simchat beit hashoevah*. When the carnival reached a certain place, people would say, 'Our ancestors in this place used to bow down to the sun; we don't any more'. Furthermore, there was a special song at the celebration for Baalei Teshuvah, those who had repented. Based on these suggestions, Rabbi Yitzhak Hutner says that the unique joy of the *simchat beit hashoevah* and of Sukkot generally is the joy at having turned over a new leaf. As he puts it 'the grief about sin, and the joy at repentance are two sides of the same coin'.

sukkah

Sukkah is the name for the sort of hut in which Jews live during the seven days of Sukkot. In Israel, where Sukkot was designed to be celebrated, people do really live in their *sukkah*, moving in their sofas, book shelves, paintings, pots and pans. Some of us even sleep in them.

The name *sukkah* comes from *sechach*, which means covering, and refers to the roof of the *sukkah*. The *sechach* is halakhically the most significant part of the *sukkah*. Whereas the walls can be made of almost any material (even from an elephant, according to the Talmud, as long as the elephant doesn't go anywhere during the festival), the *sechach* should be made from leaves, branches or other

55

non-food vegetative material no longer attached to a tree or the ground.

The halakhic significance of the *sechach* points to the *sukkah*'s spiritual meaning. We sit beneath the flimsy shade of the *sechach* to enact our trust in God's protective presence. Leaving behind most of our possessions, we affirm that our security comes from our faith, not from our toys. As we pray in the evening service, 'may God spread over us a *sukkah* of peace'.

6

Insults

As we will see in the 'Joys of Yinglish' section, Yiddish abounds in finely calibrated epithets for weakness or incompetence. Surely few if any other languages have words for schlemiel *or* schlemazel, *or take the trouble to distinguish between them. As Eskimos famously have 37 words for snow, the much-persecuted Jews have become adept at identifying precise shades of human misfortune, particularly in one another.*

Indeed 'insults' is not quite the right title for this section. The words in it certainly express a disparaging opinion, but one that is usually mixed with compassion for the poor unfortunate possessor of the trait in question.

am ha'aretz

Am ha'aretz means an ignorant or boorish person. In a culture that has always prized learning highly, it is quite a put-down to call someone an *am ha'aretz*.

The literal meaning of the phrase is 'people (*am*) of the earth (*aretz*)'. To the rabbis of the Talmud, an *am ha'aretz*, by virtue of his ignorance, was deemed likely to

57

be lax in his observance of the commandments. One common implication of this was that one couldn't count on an *am ha'aretz* separating tithes from his produce.

The rabbis argue about how you may recognize an *am ha'aretz*. Some of the possibilities are: one who doesn't say the Shema with its blessings morning and night; one who doesn't put on *tzitzit* or *tefillin*; one who has children but doesn't care to give them a Jewish education. The most stringent view is that even a person who learns Torah and Mishnah, but doesn't mix with Torah scholars, is to be considered an *am ha'aretz*: without learning face-to-face from a living sage, our knowledge is likely to be unreliable (Talmud Berakhot 47b, Sotah 22a).

Today, *am ha'artzut* (the state of being an *am ha'aretz*) has spread on a scale that the sages never imagined. Knowing what an *am ha'aretz* is, and knowing that traditionally Jews strove with all their strength to avoid being one, may be a first step to remedying this.

etzah gebber

'Thank you, but I don't need your *etzahs*', you might say more or less politely to an interfering but well-meaning family member. *Etzah* means piece of advice, plan or counsel. Giving advice seems to be a characteristic Jewish practice. There is even a Yiddish word for someone who does so habitually: *etzahgebber*.

The most famous *etzahgebber* in the Bible was Achitofel who began as adviser to King David, then crossed over to serve David's son Abshalom, when the latter revolted against his father. 'In those days, the advice [*etzah*] of Achitofel was accepted like an oracle from God' (2 Samuel 16.23). Achitofel advised Abshalom to sleep with his father's concubines, and to attack David at his most vulnerable; when he and his men were fleeing from Jerusalem. Achitofel appears to have taken great pride in his position as *etzah*-giver. When Abshalom ignored the latter piece of advice, Achitofel went home, set his affairs in order and killed himself.

Hasidim would, and sometimes still do, go to visit their rebbes hoping to receive an *etzah* and a *berakhah*, the *etzah* being a pertinent and insightful piece of advice addressed directly to the individual Hasid's spiritual situation (e.g. learn more Torah, spend more time with your children, try to be happy, etc.).

lobbes

Lobbes is a problem for students of Jewish words. On the one hand, it's well-known to most British Jews as meaning a lazybones, urchin or good-for-nothing. Who has not, at some time or other in his or her youth, been told 'Get out of bed and go to Hebrew classes right now, you *lobbes*'?

On the other hand, though people assume that *lobbes* is Yiddish, it appears in no dictionary of the language, and is almost completely unknown to American Jews of any age, whose acquaintance with Yiddish is usually deeper and more authentic than that of British Jews.

59

Some time ago, I appealed to readers of my *Jewish Chronicle* column for information regarding the word's origins. I am happy to report that the responses have been illuminating. Some have pointed out that although Americans don't have *lobbes*, they do have *shlub* or *zhlub*, which has a similar meaning and also fails to appear in Yiddish dictionaries.

Rafi Zarum of the London School of Jewish Studies creatively, but not terribly seriously, suggested that *lobbes* is an acronym for the Hebrew phrase *lo bashamayim*, 'not in heaven'. One reader posited a connection between *lobbes* and 'slob', though since the *OED* traces 'slob' to an Irish word meaning mud, this relationship appears unlikely.

Professor Ludwig Finkelstein informed me that *lobbes* is in fact a Polish word. Since he is a native Polish speaker, I am happy to take this as the authoritative derivation.

meshugge

Meshugge, meaning 'mad', 'crazy' or 'lunatic', is one of the best-known Jewish words. One need not speculate about why this is so, but *meshugge* seems to be an indispensable epithet within many Jewish families.

There are variant forms of the word. A *meshuggas* is the object of one's craziness, an obsession or *idée fixe*. You can have a *meshuggas* about cricket, communism, or that aliens are messing with your brain.

A *meshuggaimhaus* is a madhouse or slang for a psychiatric hospital. A *meshugganner* is a madman. Children who become more Jewishly observant often arouse familial fears that they are becoming *meshugganner frum* ('madly religious'). This expression is a unique creation of British Jewry. It is unknown in the USA, where they are, on the whole, more tolerant of piety.

Meshugge is a Yiddish word deriving from biblical Hebrew. It first occurs in the curses of Devarim which predict: 'You will become *meshugge* from what your eyes will see' (Deuteronomy 28.34): in other words, through witnessing the suffering that befalls the Jewish nation, people will become unhinged and deranged.

When David escapes from Saul to the kingdom of Achish, he feigns madness so that Achish will not perceive him as a threat. To this end, David dribbles into his beard and scratches at doors, prompting Achish's exclamation to his courtiers: 'Do I lack madmen (*meshuggaim*) that you bring me this one to drive me crazy (*lehishtagaya*)?' (1 Samuel 21.16).

moiser

Moiser is a word which had a long career in medieval halakhic literature. Recently it has enjoyed a revival in some circles, for interesting and unfortunate reasons.

In medieval Europe, a *moiser* was a Jew who denounced or betrayed another Jew to the Christian or Muslim authorities. (In Islamic countries it would have been pronounced *moser*.)

The word is derived from the Hebrew, meaning 'to pass or hand over'. Maimonides defines a *moiser* as someone who delivers another Jew to be killed or beaten by non-Jews, or hands over Jewish money or property. In the tight-knit medieval Jewish communities, surrounded as they often were by hostile neighbours, this was an especially heinous crime.

Whether the *moiser* acted out of greed, or out of a grudge, or to ingratiate himself with the authorities, he was ostracized from the community. Maimonides even writes that if he doesn't repent, the *moiser* has no share in the world to come.

Recently, the epithet *moiser* has been applied to Jews who denounce, or work to undermine, the State of Israel, for example by supporting academic and economic boycotts. Is this an offensive anachronism, or a recurrence of an ancient feature in Jewish life?

We may ask if the threat to Israeli Jews today is in any way comparable to the situation of beleaguered Jewish communities in medieval Europe, and if the obligations conferred by Jewish peoplehood are the same. Or has the state of Israel fundamentally changed the nature of Jewish existence among the nations?

7

Surviving *Shul*

Shul *or synagogue is a focal point of Jewish life. However it's arguably less central than temples, churches, mosques, etc. are in other religions. The observances that take place in the Jewish home are more significant to the practice and transmission of Judaism than what happens in synagogues.*

Many British and American Jews find synagogue boring. There are a number of reasons for this. The first is that very often it is boring. Services are frequently performance rather than participation; more about ceremony than spirituality, with congregants more engaged in gossip than with God. There are dynamic synagogues out there introducing singing, dancing, meditation and education to make services meaningful and spiritual, but change takes time.

A second reason is that it's often alien. Synagogue services are usually in Hebrew and the complex choreography of standing up, sitting down, bowing, kissing, opening the ark, taking out and reading from the Torah scroll, etc. can leave infrequent shul-goers feeling left out and frustrated. Language is in important part of this. Knowing when to answer 'Amen' and when to say yasher koach, *also divides initiates from outsiders.*

This short glossary may hopefully help a little with the alien nature of shul, *as I've tried to shed a little light into the spiritual depths underlying the traditional service. Unfortunately it is not a remedy for boredom. Maybe it will inspire you to help make your* shul *more exciting, or perhaps to start a new, more dynamic, one.*

Amen

Amen is a Jewish word that enjoys a level of international fame comparable to *shalom* or bagel. It signifies emphatic assent or agreement to something just said – as in 'Amen to that!'

Amen is Hebrew for 'firm', 'straight' or 'true'. It comes from the verb *aman* – to support, confirm or approve. When we say 'Amen', we confirm or support the truth of whatever we are responding to.

We say Amen virtually any time when we hear another Jew saying a blessing (but not to our own *berackah*, or to that of a child who is learning to say blessings, or when the *berakhah* is unnecessary, or when we haven't actually heard the *berakhah*).

Saying Amen, one should consciously assent to the content of the *berakhah*. It's important to take care not to say it too hastily so that we drop a sound, e.g. 'men, or cut off the end (ame-) (Talmud Berakhot 47a).

Amen is related to the word *emunah*, which means

'faith' or 'trust', and also to the word for nursemaid, *omenet*. As the Chief Rabbi likes to point out, whereas the word 'faith' evokes a mental state of belief, the Hebrew *emunah* denotes a relationship of mutual faithfulness and reliability. Faith suggests a state of mind which you either have or do not have, whereas *emunah* is a relationship that is acquired and strengthened through commitment and practice.

berakhah

We say *berakhot* from opening our eyes in the morning until closing them at night, on everything nourishing that we eat, every drop of water we drink, fragrant smells, rainbows, thunder, as well as on most of the *mitzvot* that we do.

Through *berakhot*, we acknowledge and thank God as the source of all the good we have, thereby fulfilling the words of Proverbs 3.8: 'In all your ways you shall know him'. The rabbis say that to take any physical enjoyment from the world without thanking God through a *berakhah* is tantamount to theft.

Berakhah is translated as 'blessing', though that doesn't get us very far towards understanding its meaning. (According to the *OED*, 'blessing' is derived from the Old English word meaning, 'to consecrate in blood'.) The dictionaries indicate that *berakhah* is related to the word meaning 'to select' or 'point out'.

Rabbi Aryeh Kaplan, the twentieth-century American teacher, suggests that *berakhah* is related to *beraikhah*,

65

meaning 'spring' or 'pool'. A *berakhah* acknowledges God as the ever-flowing fount and source of everything. The medieval Sefer Hakhinuch translates *barukh ata* not as 'blessed are You', but as 'You are the source of all blessing'.

The mystics teach that acknowledging God as the source of all blessing increases the flow of *berakhah* into the world. When we give a *berakhah* to someone else (for example, to our children on Friday night) we are not doing magic; rather we are opening ourselves to be channels for the influx of *berakhah*.

cohen

A *cohen* is one of the class of priests among the Jewish people. Membership is hereditary, via the father. A slew of common Jewish surnames (Cohen, Kagan, Kahane, etc.) are variations of Cohen and usually indicate that the holders are *cohanim*.

Cohen simply means priest in biblical Hebrew (as well as in Canaanite and Ugaritic). However, the Chief Rabbi, Jonathan Sacks has argued persuasively that the primary meaning of *cohen* was teacher. Just before the Torah is given, God promises that Israel will be a kingdom of priests (Exodus 19.6). This is an aspiration to universal literacy according to Rabbi Sacks, as in the ancient world only the priests could read.

The priests performed their full range of functions when the Temple stood. Today, the rights and duties of *cohanim* include being called up for the first *aliyah* to the

Torah and giving the community the priestly blessing in synagogue ('May the Lord bless you and keep you', Numbers 6.24–25).

The often-heard objection ('Why does Joe Cohen get to bless me; he's certainly not so holy') relies on a misunderstanding. The *cohanim* are servants of the people. This insight is preserved in modern Hebrew, where the verb *l'cahen* means to serve in any public capacity.

The *cohanim* bless the people 'with love'. The power of invoking blessing rests with anyone who feels love and concern for the object of their blessing, for example parents who traditionally give their children the priestly blessing on Friday night.

daven

Daven is the Yiddish word for 'pray', which has passed into common Jewish usage. But it doesn't quite have the same connotations as the English word.

Prayer is likely to conjure up images of neat, kneeling rows of worshippers, with hands pressed together and eyes turned piously heavenwards. *Daven* is more likely to evoke pictures of crowded, slightly chaotic *shtiebls*, and *shockelling* worshippers engaged in impassioned conversation, supplication or song. The word is redolent with the informality of the Yiddish-speaking world and its at-homeness with the divine. Like many of the best-known Yiddish words, the origin of *daven* is obscure. (*Lobbes* is another example, see Chapter 6.)

I know of three theories on the etymology of *daven*. The first is that it is a medieval borrowing and corruption of the Latin *divinus*, which means 'divine', or *divinar*, 'to prophesy'. The second theory, which I have heard attributed to the American Jewish studies professor Arthur Green, is a little more involved. Apparently the word *daven* means 'gift' in Lithuanian. When Jews trading in the market-places of Lithuania would break off their work in order to *daven Minchah*, the afternoon service, they would explain what they were doing by translating the word *Minchah* (which means 'offering' or 'gift', into the vernacular. The third theory is that *daven* is a contraction of the Aramaic, *d'avahan*, meaning 'of our fathers'. The Talmud attributes the three daily prayer services to the forefathers, Abraham, Isaac and Jacob.

haftarah

Chanting the *haftarah* in its minor-key trop (cantillation) is an initiation rite passed through by virtually every bar mitzvah boy. I remember investing so much effort in honing the public performance of the reading that I was entirely oblivious to its meaning until about a decade after my bar mitzvah.

The *haftarah* is a selected passage from the Prophets that is read after the week's Torah *parashah*. The *haftarah* is always thematically connected to the *parashah* except during the period between Tisha b'Av and Rosh Hashanah, when the *haftarot* are all about comfort and consolation.

The origin of the *haftarah*-reading custom is unclear. The most widely held view is that it originated during the rule of Antiochus IV (c.174–64 BCE), when Jews were forbidden to read the Torah publicly, so they read from the prophets instead. When the decree was lifted the custom continued.

On the other hand, Rabbi Samson Raphael Hirsch (1808–88) thought that the practice originated in opposition to sects which viewed only the Pentateuch as constituting the Hebrew Bible.

Haftarah is often pronounced *haftorah*, suggesting a mistaken belief that the etymology is related to Torah. Rather it is from the verb *patar*, meaning to leave, depart or conclude.

hazan

Hazan today means a prayer-leader-cum assistant rabbi, a professional who leads services on behalf of the community. In some *shuls* they still wear canonicals. *Hazanut* is the quasi-operatic musical art of *chazanim*, which reached its apogee in nineteenth-century Europe. It either moves you to tears and transports you to great spiritual heights, or bores you rigid, depending on your taste.

Hazan did not always mean this. It comes from the Hebrew word meaning 'to see'. *Hazon* in the Bible is a vision. Today, *hazai* is the modern Hebrew for weather forecaster. In the Talmudic period, a *hazan mata* was the guardian of a town. A *hazan* was also the superintendent of a school or a synagogue, where he was responsible for the smooth running of the service, assigning seats, signalling responses, etc.

The Talmud (Sukkah 51a) tells that the synagogue in Alexandria was so huge that the *hazan* would wave a flag to indicate to people when to say 'Amen'. From prayer supervisor it was a small step for the *hazan* to become the prayer leader.

A more precise term is *shaliach tzibbur* (*shatz* for short) which means agent of the community. The *shaliach tzibbur* is there to say the set prayers on behalf of those who are unable to recite them on their own (Shulhan Arukh, Orach Chayim, 124.1).

mi sheberakh

A *mi sheberakh* is the prayer said in *shul*, blessing a particular person or group. The name comes from the opening of the prayer, which means 'May the One who blesses'.

The first *mi sheberakh* appears in the Machzor Vitri (thirteenth century). This is the prayer that we still say for the wellbeing of the community, especially its leaders and *machers*. In Ashkenazi communities the custom emerged of saying individualized *mi sheberakhs* for those called up to the Torah.

This practice also continues. In many communities, it has been developed to include *mi sheberakh* for the wife and children of the *oleh* (the person called to the Torah) and extended family, too. Receiving a *mi sheberakh* is understood to confer an obligation to give charity.

Some *shuls* have a special *mi sheberakh* for those who don't talk during services. People think this is a new-fangled custom to promote decorum in our irreverent age. In fact it dates back to Rabbi Yomtov Lipmann Heller, a student of the Maharal of Prague in the seventeenth century. Some things don't change.

Jonathan Gillis of Sunderland and Jerusalem pointed out to me the ironic use of the phrase *mi sheberakh*, meaning to give somebody an earful or curse them out. In this sense, you could say, for example, 'I got home after midnight; *oy*, what a *mi sheberakh* she gave me'.

rabbi

To many British Jews, the word 'rabbi' connotes some - combination of funeral-conductor, sermon-giver, profes-sional-Jew-by-proxy and unfailing topic of conversation. There is a history to this.

British Jewry stressed the ceremonial role of its rabbis in the nineteenth century, calling them 'minister-preach-ers'. Rabbi is one of those words which needs to be returned to an earlier concept.

Rabbi means teacher, or master. Until around the destruction of the Second Temple, rabbis were those who had received the *semichah* ordination as a Master of Torah, which entitled them to sit on the Sanhedrin. This was conferred in an unbroken line stretching back to Joshua and Moses.

After the dispersion, this original *semichah* lapsed. Its eventual revival is held to be a necessary precursor for messianic times.

'Rabbi' became a term used to refer to leaders and teachers of scholarship, judgement, spiritual wisdom and counsel. The title began to be formalized in fourteenth-century Germany with the institution of a certificate giving the bearer authority to make halakhic decisions. This is the precursor of rabbinic ordination as we know it today, usually given after completing an arduous course of study.

Receiving a certificate does not transform rabbis into beings endowed with magical, priestly or sacramental powers. Like all titles, 'rabbi' is one which must be grown into through lifelong learning and striving, so that it comes ever more closely to denote the spiritual qualities of its original meaning.

Septuagint

Septuagint is the word for the first Greek translation of the Hebrew Bible. It became the basis for Bible translations into many other languages, including Ethiopian, Arabic and Armenian.

The name Septuagint, which means 70 in Latin, comes from the story of the book's creation. The Talmud, in tractate Megillah (9a–b), recounts how Ptolemy, a third-century-BCE Egyptian Pharaoh, gathered together 72

Jewish sages (close to 70), put them in 72 separate houses and demanded that each produce independently a Greek translation of the Hebrew Bible. Miraculously, they all came up with the same version. Even more remarkably, they had all decided in fifteen places to give an unusual, non-literal translation.

These fifteen points are listed by the Talmud. Most are places where a literal rendering might have given rise to theological misunderstandings. However, in one of them, (Leviticus 11.6), the Talmud says that sages translated *arnevet* as, 'short-legged animal', rather than, 'rabbit', because Ptolemy's wife's name was 'Rabbit', and the translators wanted to avoid any suspicion that they were making fun of her.

The Greek Letter of Aristeas retells this story and embellishes it with some extra details, including that six of the sages came from each tribe and that they completed their work in exactly 72 days. According to the website Wikipedia, many scholars think that the Letter of Aristeas, which purports to be a contemporary account, was written later.

Tanakh

The Talmud describes Esther writing to the sages and requesting that they 'write me for the generations', that is to say, immortalize her story by including it in the canon of the Bible (Megillah 7a). The same source discusses attempts to prove that the Book of Esther was written through divine influence – and is therefore worth including in the Bible – and was not a secular story of political intrigue as it might first appear. The Talmud also records debates about the inclusion of Kohelet (Ecclesiastes) and Song of Songs in the Bible.

These passages show that there was still some fluidity about the precise form of the Tanakh, the Hebrew Bible, in rabbinic times. Tanakh is an acronym for Torah, Nevi'im and Ketuvim: the Five Books of Moses, the Prophets and the Writings (comprising Psalms, Proverbs, the Megillot, etc.). While the Torah and Nevi'im were fixed much earlier, the Ketuvim were still being argued over in the Talmud.

Traditionally, there are 24 books of the Tanakh, though English Bibles usually come up with 39 books by adding subdivisions. (Christians called the Tanakh the Old Testament, but that term should be non-PC today, as it implies that the old has been superseded by the new.) Through canonization of the Tanakh, the Jews became the people of the Book, and the Book became the animating force of Jewish existence.

targum

Targum means 'translation'. The best-known are Onkelos's Aramaic translation of the Torah, and the Targum Yonatan of the books of the prophets.

Traditionally, the public Torah-reading on Shabbat would be accompanied by verse-by-verse translation into the Aramaic vernacular, rendered by a functionary called the *'torgaman'*, the official translator. Until recently, this was still the practice in Yemenite communities.

Interestingly, the root of the word *targum* appears to be *ragam*, meaning 'to project an object' (especially a stone.) This is parallel to the derivation of the word 'translate', which means 'to bear across', to move from one domain to another.

Judaism has an intensely ambivalent attitude to the translation of its sacred texts. The public translation of the Torah reflected the importance of the Jewish masses understanding what they heard. On the other hand, the rabbis were aware that something is always lost in translation.

Whole religions have been nourished by misunderstandings that have sprouted from accidental or deliberate mistranslations of the Torah into Greek or Latin.

The Talmud (Megillah 3a) reports that when Yonatan Ben Uziel translated the books of the prophets, the ground shuddered across an area of 400 *parasangs* and a heavenly voice demanded to know why esoteric secrets were thus being revealed. Yonatan replied that he had acted only for God's honour so that the meaning of the prophets should be made unambiguously clear.

Rabbi Abraham Isaac Kook (1865–1935) noted that the *gematria* (numerical equivalent) of *targum* is *tardemah*, meaning 'slumber'.

ArtScroll and others have helped to spread Jewish knowledge through the translation of the Talmud and other sources, but Torah study in English misses much, as if we were only half-awake.

techines

Techines (not to be confused with *techinah*, the crushed sesame-seed paste that is often eaten with hummus, which is spelt with a *tet*, not a *tav*) constituted a revolution in Jewish women's spirituality.

From the sixteenth century until our great-grandmothers' generation, Jewish women would pour out their prayers and find consolation through the *techines* collected in immensely popular books.

Originally *techines* were Yiddish translations of the Tachanun prayers (meaning supplications for grace, from the word *chen*), and other excerpts from the *siddur*. They were produced to remedy a serious gap in the religious lives of women, who generally didn't know Hebrew and so couldn't recite the set prayers with understanding.

Gradually the form was developed and embellished. One theory is that the first *techines* were created by the *firzogerins*, learned women who translated prayers into Yiddish for the benefit of the less-educated women in the community. Through their creative translations, new *techines* were born.

Throughout centuries of crisis and persecution among Eastern European Jews, the personal, heartfelt tone and the homely domestic content of the *techines* spoke to the day-to-day spiritual needs of generations of Jewish women.

Torah

'Torah' means 'teaching', the God-given wisdom by which Jews have traditionally lived. It is used in a narrow sense to denote the Chumash, the Five Books of Moses, and in a broad sense to refer to the entire body of Jewish sacred literature, evolving from the Chumash to the present day.

Torah is also classified into Torah Sh'bikhtav, the Written Torah, and Torah Sheba'al Peh, the Oral Torah. The Oral Torah originated at Sinai as an elucidation of the meaning of the Written Torah, and has developed ever since, encompassing the Mishnah, Talmud and Codes along the way.

Contrary to many mistranslations, Torah does not mean law, though it contains a lot of law within it. The word 'Torah' is better rendered as 'teaching', 'guidance' or 'direction'. Its root means to 'point' or to 'shoot an arrow'. To teach is to point out a pathway or direction.

We can barely hint here at the significance and sanctity given to Torah in Judaism, or at the rapture which the rabbis found in Torah study, or the centrality of fulfilling the Torah in the cosmic scheme.

The Torah is described as the blueprint for the creation of the universe; as a priceless treasure which God has shared with humanity; and as the direct expression of God's will for the world.

Torah has an endless capacity to renew itself, and to renew those who continuously renew their commitment to Torah. Such a reaffirmation of our commitment to Torah is the work of the holiday of Shavuot.

Vidui

The *Vidui* is the climactic section of each of the five Yom Kippur services when, bent over and contrite, we beat our breasts and enumerate the ways we have fallen short of the mark in the previous year. According to many, *Vidui* is the actualization of *teshuvah*, repentance (Maimonides, Laws of Repentance 1.1). The Torah does not clearly command repentance, but it does command *Vidui* (Numbers 5.6–7).

Our hearts may be filled with feelings of remorse and resolutions for self-improvement. But these emotions usually jostle with excuses and self-justifications. When we can articulate out loud, 'I have sinned, I have done a, b, c ...' the chaotic feelings of regret crystallize into sincere resolve.

Vidui is usually translated as confession, but this carries misleading connotations of self-abasement from other religions, and conveys no sense of the root meaning of the Hebrew word. *Vidui* in origin means to thank, praise or, most accurately in our context, to acknowledge.

The *Vidui bikkurim* is a declaration of thanksgiving to God when we bring the first fruits of the Land of Israel to Jerusalem (Deuteronomy 26.1–11).

In the *Vidui* of Yom Kippur, we peel off our customary layers of denial and rationalization to admit that we have not been who we could and should have

been. In this vein, a Hasidic rebbe said that we should
not smite our hearts punitively in the *Vidui*, but rather
knock gently upon them so that they may open up to
acknowledge the truth.

Yizkor

Yizkor is the memorial prayer for departed relatives,
which is read in synagogues on most *yomtovs* (except Rosh
Hahanah). The *shul* usually fills up right before Yizkor
and thins out shortly afterwards.

Although Judaism is not a religion based on ancestor-
worship, the desire to remember one's parents is
admirable.

There is a custom for people with two living parents to
go out during Yizkor. This is based on a superstitious fear
of attracting the attention of the evil eye, and is not
strictly necessary.

The root of the word Yizkor is *zachar*, which means 'to
remember'. Interestingly, the same Hebrew word means
'male'. This connection may be based on the traditional
role of fathers as the main transmitters of cultural
memory. It may also have to do with the active, fertilizing
effect of memory in Jewish life. Remembering inspires
action.

Recalling that we were slaves in Egypt is the spur to 38
mitzvot in the Torah (many of them to do with how we
treat marginalized members of society). The Baal Shem
Tov said: 'Memory is the secret of redemption'.

Remembering past liberations and salvations gives us faith, and inspires us to work towards future redemption.

8

The Joys of Yinglish

Leo Rosten helpfully opens his classic The Joys of Yiddish[1]
*with a short statement entitled 'What this book is not'. One of
the things that* this *book is not is a rehash of Rosten. Erudite
and entertaining as Rosten's book is, the world has moved on
since 1967 when it was first published.*

The Joys of Yiddish *celebrated the heyday of Yiddishism
in mainstream American English. A generation that had
known the slums and tenements of the Lower East Side was
still (mostly) alive and their part-nostalgic, part-rebellious
grandchildren had stormed the commanding heights of
American culture, from film to fiction and from that vantage
point injected an unparalleled quantity of Yiddish words into
the US vernacular.*

*Today, the generation of native Yiddish speakers has gone,
and the closest most of their descendants ever come to that era
is the Ellis Island museum. A good many Yiddish words are*

---

[1]   Leo Rosten, *The Joys of Yiddish* (London: Hamish Hamilton, 1967).

firmly entrenched in the language, but they are often used without the fine sense of nuance that Rosten exulted in 40 years ago.

It's still true that Yiddish is an extraordinarily rich and expressive language with, for example a remarkable range of designations for different character types. 'Little miracles of discriminatory precision are contained in the distinctions between such simpletons as a nebech, schlemiel, shmendrick *and* shnook', *as Rosten puts it. It's also poignantly evocative of the destroyed world of prewar Jewish Eastern Europe.*

I can't help feeling saddened by the brave attempts to resurrect Yiddish language, literature and culture. I wish them well. However, uprooted from the intense spirituality of the shtetl *that gave the language its vitality, I don't rate highly their chances of success. That's one reason why this book doesn't participate more extensively in that effort.*

balaboosta

Balaboostas are rather out of fashion these days, victims of feminism and women's magazines. Still, at least according to family myth, all of our grandmothers were *balaboostas* – heroic homemakers who raised large numbers of children in straitened circumstances and made real *gefilte* fish from a carp that swam about in the bath-tub.

The *balaboosta* is married to a *balaboos*, that is a home-owner, a lay person, one who works for a living – the backbone of Jewish communities. The word is a Yiddishized running together of the Hebrew words *ba'al ha'bayit*, meaning owner of a house. One of my professors at Hebrew University suggests that the English word 'boss' is related to *balaboos*, but this sounds unlikely to me.

Balaboos can be turned into an adjective, *balabatish*, which means solid, homely and dependable. In certain *Haredi* circles it has slightly pejorative connotations. A *balabatish sevarah* is a plodding or pedestrian line of Talmudic argument, lacking the originality and analytical precision to which those in full-time yeshivah learning aspire. (However, the phrase does reflect the impressive reality that religious *balabatim* did, and still do, devote significant time to Torah study.)

In Pirkei Avot, the Ethics of the Fathers (2.20), God is described as a *ba'al ha'bayit* in the following homely metaphor for life: 'The day is short, the work is great, the workers are lazy, the reward is much, and the *ba'al ha'bayit* is urgent'.

chutzpah

'Chutzpah' was a famous Jewish word even before Professor Alan Dershowitz wrote a book with that title a few years ago.

Dershowitz made an argument for being the sort of assertive, confident, in-your-face Jew he believes one can and should be in the USA today. The book, and its insouciantly Jewish title, tell all you need to know about the differences between American and British Jews.

Historically, 'chutzpah' (usually translated as 'boldness', 'barefacedness' or 'impudence') has been a necessary Jewish trait. It has helped us to succeed as immigrants and outsiders.

The word is at least Mishnaic (1,900 years old) in origin. Its root is the Hebrew *chatzaf*, which means 'peel off', or 'bare'. Its Talmudic connotations are not wholly positive. A court which attempts to function with only two judges, instead of the usual three, is called a 'Beth Din *chatzuf*', an arrogant court (Sanhedrin 2b).

The Talmud says that the generation preceding the coming of the Messiah will be one in which 'chutzpah prevails' (Sotah 49b). Since it also says of that generation that truth will be absent, and God-fearing people will be ridiculed, we can see that chutzpah here is not entirely a compliment.

However, some of the Hasidic rebbes saw 'chutzpah' as an important spiritual quality. Rebbe Nachman of Bratzlav writes that when we think of our flaws and imperfections, which keep us far from God, we can feel like giving up on trying to come close to him. At these moments 'chutzpah' is necessary, in order to pray and to continue to strive to approach God, despite everything.

gevalt

The word *gevalt* is the linchpin in the punchlines of innumerable Jewish standup routines. Just to have Mrs

Cohen cry *'Oy gevalt'* at the slightest provocation is considered to be the summit of ethnic humour.

Gevalt! in Yiddish means 'help', or 'emergency', but it has come to be a useful exclamation for any untoward occurence, such as dropping a milk spoon into chicken soup. In German, *Gevalt* means force or violence. Thus the word came to be used as a cry of protest and alarm by Jews at violence directed against them. (Weinrich's *Yiddish–English Dictionary* gives *'Shema Yisrael'* as a synonym for *Gevalt*!) *'Schrei Gevalt'* means to raise a cry of protest against some anti-Jewish outrage, as in the recent debate about whether *'schrei-ing gevalt'* is the best way of responding to anti-Jewish bias in the media.

In recent years the word *'gevalt'* has become a multi-purpose expression in neo-Hasidic circles, meaning the opposite of help. This is almost entirely due to Shlomo Carlebach, the singing rabbi, who would frequently exclaim *'gevaldig!'*, or *'mamash gevalt!'* about a Hasidic master or teaching, meaning amazing, incredible, on a truly sublime spiritual level. This parallels the shift in meaning of 'bad' and 'wicked' to mean something like 'remarkably impressive', a phenomenon for which I'd be interested to hear an explanation.

goyishe naches

If some Jew or other has received a knighthood or a Nobel prize, another Jew, of a more traditional sensibility, might dismiss such honours as *goyishe naches*. This means,

LET'S SCHMOOZE: JEWISH WORDS TODAY

roughly, meaningless sources of prestige and satisfaction that non-Jews might enjoy, but Jews should know better than to take any pride in, as opposed to Yiddishe *naches*, which comes from such sources as helping old ladies across the road, or one's grandchildren. (But what if one's grandchild wins a Nobel Prize?)

The phrase comes from goy, the biblical world for nation, as in 'two nations are within your womb' (Genesis 25.23), which later came to denote non-Jewish nations in particular; and *naches*, which means calm, satisfaction or peace of mind. Around the time of Israel Independence Day, some parts of the *Haredi* community lump together flags, governments, armies and memorials for fallen soldiers as *goyishe naches*, as if the apparatus of national sovereignty is permanently outside the reach of Jewish values, rather than being a sphere that may be infused with ethical content.

There's undoubtedly a taint of chauvinism about this expression. However, the disdainful refusal to be impressed by the power and prestige of the nations among which we've been a small minority has done much to enable our survival. The flip side of the sense of superiority is a focus on the things that really matter.

hekdesh

Hekdesh is a Yiddish–Hebrew word meaning, in popular parlance, a 'big mess', as in, 'Clear up your bedroom right now; it looks like a *hekdesh*'. (In truth, I've heard it used colloquially only in the USA, where Yiddish was not deliberately purged from Eastern European immigrants as it was in the UK.)

Originally, *hekdesh* meant something very different. Money or objects pledged to the Temple were designated as *hekdesh*.

One could dedicate *hekdesh* either to the upkeep and maintenance of the Temple, or to the specific sacrifices. The owner of an object could make something *hekdesh* simply by saying so; even in some circumstances just by mentally dedicating it. Once it was rendered *hekdesh* in this way it could not be used for any other purpose until it was formally redeemed.

At a certain point after the destruction of the Temple, the term came to refer to donations of objects to the community, particularly for use by the poor.

Hekdesh was another word for a *gamach*, that is a repository of expensive items, such as wedding dresses, that were lent out to those unable to afford their own.

The Temple no longer stood, but this was an analogous way of contributing to the public good. *Hekdeshim* thus became storehouses for all of the community's junk, and hence paved the way for the word's meaning to morph into 'mess'.

kvetch

Kvetch is another Jewish word on the verge of making the big breakthrough into standard English. Most people have an idea that it means to complain in a way which is assumed to be particularly Jewish, but few realize what a versatile word it is.

The etymology of *kvetch* is the key to understanding its range of uses. Kvetch is Yiddish from German, deriving in turn from the medieval French, *esquasher*. It is thus a cousin, sharing a common lineage with the English word squash.

This shows why one can *kvetch* a bottle of tomato ketchup to get the last drops out, or *kvetch* a family with three kids into a Mini. It also helps explain why the rabbi can *kvetch* out his sermon for a whole half an hour, or why a *kvetch* can also be a stretched, forced or far-fetched interpretation, as in, 'It's a good book, but the author's attribution of the poems to Shakespeare was really a *kvetch*', or, 'He managed to *kvetch* anti-Semitic implications from a perfectly harmless statement'.

The more familiar uses of *kvetch* follow figuratively. Using it as a verb, you can say, 'Our 3-year-old *kvetches* to have tomato ketchup with whatever food you put in front of him'. As an adjective, 'The baby was so *kvetchy*, we didn't sleep all night'. Or as a noun, 'It's not surprising that she's such a *kvetch* after the divorce and everything else she's gone through'. With a bit of a *kvetch* you can even make it adverb: 'Just try not to talk so *kvetchily*, OK?'

lamedvovnik

Lamedvovnik is a popular Yiddish word for one who does exceptional good deeds quietly, without seeking public acclaim or recognition, such as the non-religious Israeli taxi-driver who called me this morning to let me know that he'd found my wallet in his cab.

The word means 'one of the thirty-six'. It derives from the legend, elaborated over centuries, that the world is sustained by the righteous actions of 36 hidden, just people. They are so modest that nobody knows who they are.

One can trace the origin of the legend from Talmudic stories in which the most unlikely and unassuming people turn out to have extraordinary merit. In one episode (Ta'anit 22a), Elijah stands in the market-place, pointing out to an astonished rabbi the unlikely looking character among the passers-by who are assured of a place in the world to come. These examples of virtue include a jailer and two jesters.

The number 36 seems to have been introduced by the Talmudic Rabbi Abbaye, who based it on an interpretation of the verse, 'Happy are they that hope for him' (Isaiah 30.18): (the numerical value of the word for 'him' being 36).

The power of the legend of the *lamedvovniks* is that we never know who they are. We cannot fathom the true nature of those around us or pass judgement on them. Maybe you, or your neighbour, or my taxi-driver, are among those hidden heroes.

maiseh

Maiseh, (or *ma'aseh* in Hebrew) is Yiddish for a story. It's best known when conjoined with the Yiddish word for grandma in the compound *bubbamaiseh*, meaning a folktale of doubtful veracity (though my grandmother, if she's reading this, should not take it as in any way impugning the truthfulness of her stories).

The Hebrew *ma'aseh* literally means act or deed, and comes from the word for making or doing. *Ma'aseh Bereishit* is the story or act of Creation. A *ma'aseh sh'hayah* means a story that really happened. The great Hebrew writer S.Y. Agnon (1888–1970) begins many of his short fictions with those words. It is interesting that a story is synonymous with doing.

In a culture based on the Bible, which is long on narrative and short on description, stories are primarily accounts of acts rather than of flabby introspection. In the Talmud, a *ma'aseh* has the force of a legal argument. A story recording the deed of a famous rabbi may be cited to support a halakhic argument in favour of that action. The rabbinic emphasis on the value of action is further accentuated by the Talmudic phrase for spiritual giants, *anshei ma'aseh*, literally meaning 'people of deeds'.

maven

Maven has so thoroughly entered English (particularly in the USA), that most people don't realize that it comes from Hebrew and Yiddish. A *maven* is an expert in something. You can be a political *maven*, a car *maven*, a movie *maven* or a make-up *maven*.

A recent book of popular social psychology, *The Tipping Point*,[1] categorizes the type of people you need to spread a product or idea: among them are 'connectors' (people who know a lot of people) and *mavens*, people who thoroughly understand the product. (Maven is also the name of the best Jewish Internet search engine.)

The origin of *maven* is the Hebrew and Yiddish word *mavin*, which simply means 'to understand'. In Jewish esoteric literature, whether philosophical or kabbalistic, you see the phrase *ha'maven yavin*, literally 'the one who understands will understand'.

This occurs often in Nachmanides' commentary on the Torah. When he alludes to a kabbalistic secret, he will say as an aside, '*ha-maven yavin*', which means roughly 'I've given enough information for an initiate into kabbalah to grasp my meaning, but not enough for a non-initiate to understand, or even worse, to misunderstand what I'm saying'.

Ha-maven yavin has also entered popular use in *frum* circles, to denote an allusion to insider knowledge, ideas or jokes. A student once e-mailed me to voice concerns about the religious well-being of another student, concluding 'I don't want to be a Ned Flanders [the

---

[1]   Malcolm Gladwell *The Tipping Point* (New York, 2000).

sanctimonious neighbour in The Simpsons] or anything. *Ha-maven yavin'*.

naches

Naches is another of those Jewish words with no precise English equivalent. The historian Paula Hyman defines it as 'a unique mix of pride, joy and gratification'. When those we care about (usually children and grandchildren) achieve something remarkable (and usually public, like getting into Oxford, or appearing on *Pop Idol*) we say that we *schepp naches* from them. (*Schepp*, not *schlepp*, as I've laboured in these pages to show.)

An investigation into the roots of the word shows that this usage is not quite right. *Naches* literally means calm, tranquility or peace, from the verb *nach* meaning to rest or put down. Ecclesiastes 4.6 tells us, 'better a handful with calm (*naches*) than both hands with labour and striving after wind', in other words, better to have a little with contentment than a lot with contention. *Nachat ruach* means satisfaction or peace of mind; we can give *nachat ruach* to people close to us or even, according to the Talmud, to God when we do that which pleases him (Berakhot 17a).

From this we can see that *naches* as applied to children and grandchildren is more accurately used for the lasting peace of mind we gain from seeing that our efforts and struggles to raise them have borne fruit – when we see that they've turned out stable, happy and with good values. *Naches* is more properly applied not to some fleeting public feat but to the achievement of bringing up a *mensch*.

oy veh

'*Oy veh*', a venerable Jewish exclamation of dismay, beloved of Borsht-belt comedians, has remarkably ancient origins. *Oy* appears in the Talmud and Midrash. Explaining how Datan and Aviram became involved in Korach's rebellion because they were camped close to Korach, the Midrash Tanchuma exclaims, '*Oy* to the wicked, and *oy* to his neighbour'. Similarly in Berakhot 61a the Talmud, lamenting the painfulness of our struggle with the evil inclination cries '*Oy l'yitzri v' oy l'yotzri*' (*Oy* to my inclination and *oy* to my Maker, if I follow the evil inclination.)

Indeed the roots of *oy* as a Jewish distress call are probably even older. In several places in the book of Isaiah, *hoy* has the same meaning as *oy* assumes later on (as in '*hoy*, a sinful nation ...' (Isaiah 1.4.)

Veh simply means pain, ache or sorrow in German and Yiddish. Thus '*Oy veh*' means '*Oy*, it hurts'.

Related exclamations are '*veh iz mir*' (woe is me) and *Oy v'voy*, which appears to be an alliterative variation of *Oy veh*. *Oy v'voy* also has a long history. In the sixteenth century the Maharal of Prague used *Oy v'voy* to bemoan the misplaced emphasis on *pilpul* in the Talmudic learning of his day (Netivot Hatorah, Chapter 5).

One of the many heartwarming things about sending your children to a religious nursery in Jerusalem is to hear a 4-year-old say '*Oy v'voy*' when the milk spills.

schmooze

Another Jewish word that is perennially misused. In English (as opposed to American) Yiddish, *schmooze* has slightly dishonourable connotations. It can imply flattery, insincerity, conversation with a hint of manipulation about it. One might read in the papers, 'The Prime Minister was seen *schmoozing* potential party donors'. Or one might take clients out to lunch to '*schmooze* them up'. In Yiddish, however, these negative connotations are absent. *Schmooze* means to chat. It's without ulterior motive. The Musar *yeshivot*, which focused on individual ethical development, instituted the *schmooze* as a regular part of the curriculum.

The Musar schmooze was an informal talk given by the rabbi of the yeshivah most respected for his moral qualities. It aimed to inspire, challenge and support students on their path of growth to be better people. The *schmooze* was marked by sincerity and directness, not ingratiation or flattery.

The root of the word *schmooze* is the Hebrew word *shema*. *Shema* means 'hear'. It is also the name of our most famous and fundamental prayer, declaring our faith in the one God. The *Shema* (or at least the first line) must be said with conviction and intention.

The Talmud tells us: 'Let your ears hear what your mouth declares'. We need to speak the words of our faith sincerely and open our ears and our hearts to receive what we say. This is speech of a kind which is very far removed from the inauthenticity which *schmooze* has come to connote.

shmatter

Shmatter is one of those useful Yiddish words with a skein of interconnected meanings. Its primary sense means rag, as in 'Don't just stand there like a *schlemiel*; take a *shmatter* and wipe it up'. From here it comes to mean torn, messy or inferior clothing, as in, 'He goes around in *shmatters* just to upset his mother'.

Most of us had forebears in the *shmatter* business at one time or another. Strictly speaking, this was the trade of those who collected the unused rags from clothes factories, sorted them and sold them back to the companies. (Kirk Douglas's autobiography was called *The Rag Man's Son*.) However, it came to include the whole garment industry. My grandfather tailored men's suits and that was part of the *shmatter* business too.

Metaphorically, it comes to mean someone of low confidence or self-esteem, e.g., 'After being yelled at like that I just feel like a *shmatter*'. '*Shmattered* out' means chronically low in self-esteem. To treat someone like a *shmatter* is to behave towards them with deep disrespect.

Shmatters have long since made way for detergent-filled wipes, and the ragmen's grandchildren have become novelists, rabbis and film-stars, but the word *shmatter* remains a living link with the world of our ancestors.

shtadlan

Premodern Jewish communities all had *shtadlanim*. Modern Jewish communities all have them too, though often unaware of it. *Shtadlan* comes from the Hebrew verb *l'hishtadel*, meaning 'to endeavour', or 'strive', which derives in turn from the root *shadal*, meaning 'to persuade, entice or solicit'.

The *shtadlan* was the community's official intercessor and lobbyist with the non-Jewish authorities. *Shtadlanim* needed a command of the local vernacular and culture, familiarity with the legal and political systems, negotiating skill, and the ability generally to cut an impressive figure in the wider world.

Sometimes the *shtadlan* was a paid communal position; sometimes he earned his role by virtue of wealth or connections.

Even today, the notion persists that only select individuals are rich, cultured or prestigious enough to represent Jewish interests to the non-Jewish world.

In one of the few references to *shtadlanim* in traditional literature, Rabbi Isaiah Horowitz (1565–1630), in his book *Shnei Luchot Habrit*, is obviously embarrassed by the obsequiousness towards Gentile authority which the institution of *shtadlanut*, and by extension, diaspora existence, engender.

He cites examples of apparent grovelling by *shtadlanim* in the Bible, such as Nehemiah and Esther ('If the king thinks it good . . .' Esther 5.4). In a stunning rereading, he asserts that the king whose favour is really being implored is not the non-Jewish ruler, but the King of Kings. Horowitz concludes: 'This is what should be the intention in the heart of every *shtadlan*'.

shtick

Shtick has long been mainstream English in the USA and is now making its way into British use. In colloquial parlance, it means, roughly, personal, idiosyncratic or trademark behaviour with which someone is particularly associated.

You might say that wearing kabbalistic symbols is today part of Madonna's *shtick*, or that having a gentleman in a crimson jacket with a booming voice make the announcements at wedding receptions is part of Anglo-Jewish *shtick*. If you think that someone's behaviour is idiosyncratic to the point of self-indulgence, you could call it *shticky*.

Shtick is Yiddish, defined in my dictionary as 'piece, pranks, whims or capricious carrying on'. It derives from the German *stück*, meaning 'piece'. It's often used in this sense among traditional Jews as the diminutive *shtickel*, 'a little piece'. You can ask someone to pass you a *shtickel* of bread or say a *shtickel* of Torah, that is, a short *dvar* Torah.

At traditional Jewish weddings where the focus of the guests is on helping the bride and groom to be as happy as possible, *shtick* has come to mean the entertainment that the couple's friends put on for them during the dancing. Fire-eating, juggling, red noses, cross-dressing, handstands, break-dancing ... All come into the category of *shtick*, and are ways in which guests try to do the mitzvah of *'m'sameakh hatan v'kalah'*, 'bringing joy to the newly married couple'.

tzores

of *Tzores* is another of those well-worn Yiddish words which conjures up tiresome images from mainstream culture of pantomime Jewish mothers clutching their foreheads and inveighing about the quantity of *tzores* in their lives.

Tzores is hard to translate precisely, but roughly speaking it's a combination of trouble, distress, calamity, plight, woe and aggravation. It can be used of a wide range of individual hardships, such as poverty, illness and depression. In the Bible, it's used on numerous occasions to mean personal trouble and suffering: e.g. 'God will answer you in your time of trouble' (Psalm 20.2).

From the Talmud onwards, *tzores* is also used to describe the persecutions that were the recurrent collective lot of the Jewish people in exile. *Tzarot* follow, one upon the other, so that 'the later *tzarot* cause the earlier ones to be forgotten' (Talmud, Berachot 13a).

Torah study was one of the key activities that enabled us to retain equanimity in the face of the reversals, as in the saying, 'Whoever neglects the study of Torah, will have no strength to face the day of trouble' (Berachot 63a).

Tzores comes from the Hebrew word meaning narrow. In *tzores* our feelings are constricted or straitened.

The very use of this word for suffering implies that it is a temporary state which will in time be replaced by breadth and openness, as it says in Psalm 118.5: 'I called out to God in my straits, and he answered me with expansiveness'.

9

Who is a Jew?

One of the more regrettable features of Jewish community life is a tendency to factionalism. Perhaps it's the downside of the great Jewish tradition of passionate debate for the sake of Heaven. The famous joke of the Jew marooned on the desert island who builds two synagogues – one that he prays in and one that he wouldn't be seen dead in – reflects our long history of disputatiousness.

It may or may not be a comfort to learn that it's been this way for at least 2,000 years. In the first century there were Pharisees, Sadducees, Essenes and proto-Christians (the latter beginning as a schismatic Jewish sect.) The Middle Ages saw Karaites pitted against Rabbanites, as well as Maimonideans versus anti-Maimonideans. During the eighteenth century, Mitnagdim confronted Hasidim, with both united against the Maskilim. The nineteenth century spawned the Reform, Conservative and Orthodox denominations, and the twenty-first has already given birth to post-denominationalists, New Jews and Jubus.

This partial list of labels may be a little help in navigating the contemporary Jewish world. It comes with a health warning: not to treat these intra-Jewish distinctions as seriously as the bearers of the labels do!

edah

'How long with this evil *edah* who are complaining against me' (Bamidbar 14.27) exclaims Moses in exasperation after the episode of the spies. The rabbis understand the word *edah* as referring here to the group of ten spies who discouraged the people by testifying falsely to the invincibility of the inhabitants of the land.

Edah is loosely used to mean a community; for example, the Edah Haredit is the Haredi community, and 'Edot Hamizrach' is the politically correct term for Jews from North Africa, Spain and the Middle East who used to be known as Sephardi. However, etymology gives a more precise definition. *Edah* is related to the word *ed*, meaning witness. From this, we see that an *edah* is a group or community of people that bears witness. By comparing the use of *edah* in the story of the spies to its use in Vayikra, 18, 'and I shall be made holy within the *edah* of Israel', the rabbis learn that ten is the minimum number for events which publicly sanctify God, which is the root of the concept of a *minyan*.

The Jewish people are sometimes referred to as 'Edat Yisrael'. The point of our being in the world is to bear witness to God, through our way of life, and through our extraordinarily improbable, even miraculous continued

101

existence. 'You are my witnesses, says God' (Isaiah 43.12). On this, the midrash comments boldly, 'If you are my witnesses, then I am God; if you are not my witnesses I am – as it were – not God'.

frum

If you're Jewishly observant you are liable to be called a *frummer*. In Britain you may be called a *meshugganer frummer*. (Readers may be surprised to learn that this charming phrase with its implicit connection between religiosity and mental illness is in use nowhere else in the Jewish world.) In America *frummie* means sanctimoniously *frum*. *Frumkeit* is the way of life of the *frum*, and Frumster is a dating website for the *frum* which boasts hundreds of successful matches.

I haven't been able to trace when *frum* entered the Jewish lexicon, but it does not appear to have been before the enlightenment. My theory is that it only became necessary to coin a colloquial expression for a religious Jew when significant numbers of Jews became *frei* (the opposite of *frum*, denoting those who had made themselves 'free' from the responsibilites of Jewish observance).

Frum is Yiddish from the German, *froom*, meaning religious or pious. Interestingly, *froom* also means 'steady', when used of a horse. This may not seem to be a very flattering word to apply to Torah-observant Jews. However, the underlying idea seems to be that steadiness and reliability, underrated virtues today, are essential in those who would commit themselves to a *frum* way of life. This jives with our notion of *emunah* as faithfulness; that Jewish belief and practice are best conceived of as ongoing faithfulness to a relationship and a covenant.

Haredi

'Haredi' is the self-definition of those groups of Orthodox Jews who tend to live in enclosed communities and carefully regulate their interaction with the secular world and strive assiduously to learn Torah and fulfil *mitzvot*.

'Haredi' is preferable to the mainstream media's designation of such Jews as 'Ultra-Orthodox', with its implication of their having completely gone off the deep end.

Indeed in the mouth of some news outlets, the term 'Ultra-Orthodox' seems to me to have a whiff of *Der Sturmer* about it.

The word *haredi* means, literally, 'those who tremble or are afraid'. When Isaac discovered that he had blessed Jacob and not Esau, he trembled (*harad*) very much. In a phrase that is close to our contemporary usage, Isaiah addresses the God-fearing as 'those who tremble (*haredim*) at his word' (Isaiah 66.5.) *Haredim* there signifies not so much fear, as anxiousness to fulfil God's will.

Although there is an early modern ethical work named 'Sefer Haredim', it seems that only in the twentieth century did the word begin to be used generically to describe a broad swathe of Jewry.

Just as the word 'black' has rightly replaced pejorative expressions such as 'nigger' and 'coloured', so too 'Haredi' should be used instead of the prejudicial 'Ultra-Orthodox.'

Jewish

'Jew', *Juif, Jude*, 'Yid', etc. are all Europeanized versions of 'Yehudi', which refers to someone from the tribe or region of Yehudah, Judah. How did the name of one of Jacob's sons and the Twelve Tribes come to denote the whole people of Israel? It happened late in the biblical period. After the death of King Solomon, his kingdom split into two parts; the Kingdom of Judah which comprised the tribes of Judah and Benjamin, and the Kingdom of Israel, made up of the other ten tribes.

Around 700 BCE Sennacherib, King of Assyria, carried away the ten tribes into exile and they were effectively dissolved and known thereafter as the Ten Lost Tribes. (Many cranks throughout history have claimed to find, or to be, their descendants.) From then on, 'Yehudi' came to mean the collectivity of Jews in the Land of Israel.

This usage received a new twist when Nebuchadnezzar, King of Babylon, exiled the remaining two tribes in 586 BCE. The exiled people were known as 'Yehudim'. For example, in the Book of Esther (2.5), Mordecai is called an 'ish Yehudi', and then we're told that he was a scion of

Benjamin. Rashi explains that even so, the Megillah calls him a Yehudi because Judah was the larger of the two tribes.

The name stuck.

Many have linked the reasons for Judah's naming with some essential feature of the Jewish people. 'This time I will thank (*odeh*) God', his mother Leah says (Genesis 29.35). To be a Jew is to know how to give thanks.

New Jews

'We are the New Jews, out, loud, proud, and in your face. We are the "Hello, I'm Jewish" generation.' So begins Londoner Sasha Frieze's 'New Jew Manifesto'.

She's describing a large-scale phenomenon of the past five to ten years that has caused no little bafflement and concern to Jewish sociologists and communal leaders here and in the USA.

New Jews are usually (but not always) young, at ease with their Jewishness and happy to express it in a range of eclectic, unpredictable and self-chosen forms: Jewish film, going to get bagels at 2 a.m., sponsored environmental cycle rides in Israel, or whatever.

The headache for communal leaders is that New Jews are not terribly interested in the organized Jewish community. They tend not to go to *shul* much, Israel is not a big part of their identity and they are impatient with the 'is-it-good-for-the-Jews' insularity that they perceive in the establishment (the lampooning of which in Jonny Geller's recent book *Yes, but is it good for Jews?* makes it a New Jew phenomenon).

Today's New Jews are not the first to claim the title. The founding generation of Israeli pioneers also called themselves the New Jews, taking up the confident, outdoorsy, self-reliant values of the Hebrew-speaking *sabra*, in opposition to the bookish, fearful, inward-looking passivity that they saw in the Old Jews of the diaspora.

Twenty-first-century New Jews believe that, with anti-Semitism basically a thing of the past, the inner freedom and self-confidence that the early Zionists aspired to can now be enjoyed in the diaspora. I would not bet the studio flat in Cricklewood on it.

10

From *Brit* to Burial: Jewish Life-cycle Events

Life-cycle events are occasions when less observant Jews and non-Jews have a brush with Jewish religious life. Along with the paper or velvet yarmulke respectfully donned at the circumcision or the graveside comes a plethora of Hebrew words that accompany, illuminate or sometimes confuse the event for the uninitiated. It can be baffling to be asked to read a sheva berakha *at a friend's wedding, and downright alarming when the rabbi hands you a pair of nail scissors and asks you to perform* keriyah *before a relative's funeral.*

Non-observant Jews often have a particular respect for Jewish rituals around death and mourning. Whatever their views on religion in general they want to do the right thing there. A friend of mine once rather harshly described this phenomenon in a small provincial Jewish community as 'bordering on necrophilia'. Much as one might want rituals around life to be observed, as much as those dealing with death, this attitude does speak of a deep reverence for ancestors and tradition that has done much to perpetuate Judaism.

Hopefully this short lexicon of life-cycle words will help make readers' encounters with these events more real, and perhaps open a window on the rich meanings that lie behind the words and practices.

bar/bat mitzvah

A bar or bat mitzvah is a Jewish coming-of-age ceremony held at 13 for boys and 12 for girls. It is an excuse to have a big, Harry Potter-themed party; the spiritual aspect tends to be forgotten. (A lot of *bar*, not much *mitzvah*, as the old rabbinic line has it.) The event which is meant to celebrate one's entry into the world of adult Jewish responsibilty is very often a grand graduation party marking one's exit from Jewish communal life.

Bar or bat mitzvah means son or daughter of the commandments. At bar mitzvah age, you become morally responsible for your actions, including those religious obligations which devolve upon a Jewish adult. The notion that 13 is the age of responsibility is an ancient one. According to the Midrash, at that age, Jacob and Esau went their separate ways, one to the study-house, and the other to temples of idolatry. The Talmud connects the ages of 13 and 12 to the onset of puberty. At this point one becomes responsible for one's desires.

Although the ages of bar and bat mitzvah were fixed long ago, the ceremonies we have are recent. Only in the fifteenth century do we begin to hear of bar mitzvah celebrations where the boy is publicly called to the Torah and gives a *derasha*, and only in the nineteenth century did bat mitzvahs for girls develop.

You don't 'become a man' the day you turn 13. The titles 'man' and 'woman' (like 'rabbi' and 'doctor") are not entities that one is miraculously transformed into with the conferring of a label. Rather they are invitations to begin growing into the title.

One key to a meaningful bar or bat mitzvah is to look to the future. A good idea is to make a specific, self-chosen, achievable commitment towards some sort of Jewish involvement over the coming years, e.g. continuing Jewish education, volunteer work, visiting Israel, etc.

brit

The word *brit* is most widely known as the name for the circumcision ceremony which Jewish boys undergo, normally at eight days old. It is also called the *brit shel Avraham Avinu*, after Abraham to whom the *mitzvah* of circumcision was first given (Genesis 17.10) and *brit milah*. (*Milah* also means word. Exploring the connection between these ideas would require another article.)

The word *brit* is literally translated as circle, ring or chain. From these senses the main meaning of *brit* derives: *brit* as covenant, a binding agreement between two parties. *Brit* in this sense is at the heart of Judaism. God made covenants with Abraham, Isaac and Jacob, and with the Jewish people as a whole at Mount Sinai, and on the plains of Moab as they were about to enter the Land of Israel. The content of the covenant was that we agreed to be partners with God in perfecting the world, while God agreed to maintain us as his eternal, chosen people.

In his profound writings on the subject, Chief Rabbi Sacks shows how the idea of a *brit* was one of the most original Jewish contributions to world thought. As he puts it: 'A *brit* is made when free agents, respecting one another's freedom, bind themselves by a mutual promise to work together, to be loyal to one another, and to achieve together what neither can achieve alone.'[1] It is not an agreement to be set aside when convenient, but one which constitutes who we are. Marriage at its best is the most tangible everyday example of *brit*.

Hatan

The time-honoured tradition of the Hatan Torah and Hatan Bereshit giving a *kiddush* on Shabbat Bereshit echoes a custom from the Middle Ages when those two dignitaries would make a feast for the community. (Like most of the Simchat Torah celebrations that we have today, this originated a mere 600–700 years ago.)

Why is the word *Hatan* used to describe the two people called up to say the blessings on the last section of the old year's Torah reading and the first section of the new cycle? *Hatan* means a bridegroom or a son-in-law. It comes from the verb meaning to tie, connect or covenant.

---

[1]   Jonathan Sacks, *To Heal a Fractured World*, (London, 2005).

According to Jastrow's *Talmudical Dictionary*, this derives from the Assyrian word, *chatanu*, meaning to protect, obviously a function of bridegrooms in ancient societies.

A *Hatan* becomes tied, connected and covenanted to his new family. So too, the idea of the Hatan Torah may be that the person so honoured becomes deeply connected to the Torah as if married to it.

But *Hatan* has another range of associations as well. It's applied to winning all kinds of distinction; *hatan haneshef*, for example, means a guest of honour.

Hatan Pras Hanobel means a Nobel Prize winner. The Hatan Torah and Hatan Bereshit are the stars of the day in this sense also.

huppah

A *huppah* is the canopy made of cloth and poles under which a Jewish couple gets married. It has also become synonymous with the wedding ceremony itself (as in 'Huppah, 4 p.m. ... Carriages 11 p.m.'; both being ancient words with a venerable place on Anglo-Jewish wedding invitations, though *huppahs* seem to have long outlived carriages in their practical usefulness.)

The word *huppah* appears in the Bible. The sunrise is compared to 'a bridegroom coming out of his *huppah*.' (Psalm 19.6). There is, however, a disagreement about the etymology of the word. Some authorities claim that it is derived from the word *hafah*, meaning to cover or hide (as in Esther 6.12), where Haman emerges from the king's banquet *hafui rosh*, with his head covered. Others maintain that the root is *hafaf*, which means to cover in the sense of to protect (as in Devarim 33.12, where the tribe of Benjamin is blessed that it will dwell permanently under God's protection.)

The *huppah* symbolically represents the couple's first home. By standing together under a *huppah* they publicly enact their living together. There are two parts to the wedding ceremony; the first, *kiddushin* (betrothal), is completed through the man giving a ring to the woman. The second, *nesuin* (marriage), is accomplished by the couple standing under the *huppah* (or, according to some authorities by their being alone together for a few minutes after the ceremony.)

keriyah

Keriah, tearing one's clothes, is one of the most distinctive Jewish mourning practices. It can also seem one of the strangest. As a rabbi, it can be pretty uncomfortable to try to persuade an unprepared and traumatized mourner to rip their clothing at the graveside. As the mourner, it must be far more so.

Keriah comes from the verb meaning to rip or rend. Jewish law requires mourners for close relatives to tear an item of clothing on hearing of the death, or at the funeral. For a parent, the tear should be made by the mourner and be plainly visible. For other close relatives, it may be done by someone else and need not show. For parents, a torn garment should be worn the whole *shivah*.

We read of mourners tearing their clothing in the Bible. Jacob rips his cloak when he hears the (false) report of his son Joseph's demise (Genesis 37.34), and David tears his clothes when he receives news of King Saul's death (2 Samuel 1.11).

Keriah is a ritualized expression for the anger and grief that a mourner feels. In some cultures, the deceased's property is destroyed; in others, mourners mutilate themselves. Judaism forbids these excessive practices, but recognizes and channels the human instincts that provoke them. The *halakhah* of *keriyah* which can appear alien gives vent to a natural impulse. Thus expressing feelings of grief is said to be healing.

levayah

A *levayah* (or *levoyoh* in Ashkenazi pronunciation) is a funeral. The root of the word, which means 'accompanying', is *lavah*, to join or be connected. In the Bible, Leah calls her third son Levi, because she hopes that 'this time, my husband will be connected to me, *yilaveah ishi*', (Genesis 29.34).

Levayat hamet, 'accompanying the dead person' on his or her final journey, is one *mitzvah* accomplished by attending a funeral. (The other is comforting the mourners.) In so doing, one gives honour to the one who has died. *Levayat hamet* is a way in which we can express *hesed*, loving-kindness (Maimonides, Laws of Mourning, 14.1). The *hesed* performed for someone who has died is called '*hesed shel emet*', kindness done for its own sake, with no expectation that the beneficiary will ever repay us.

A happier kind of *levayah* is involved in the *mitzvah* of hospitality. Part of the *mitzvah* is to escort one's guests on the first part of their journey. In more perilous times and places, one reason for this was to protect them: the Talmud says that failing to accompany guests is tantamount to shedding blood.

Today, though, walking a little with one's guests is another way of making them feel welcome, and demonstrating that one isn't desperate to get rid of them!

shalom bayit

Sh'lom bayit, the proper Hebrew pronunciation of *shalom bayit*, is a key concept in traditional Jewish marriage. Literally meaning 'peace or harmony in the home', it also refers to any practice or behaviour likely to promote those ends.

You might say for example, 'We tried not to go out separately in the evenings during our first year of marriage for *sh'lom bayit*', or 'I had to give up mud-wrestling when I got married – a *sh'lom bayit* issue'.

Sh'lom bayit is already prominent in rabbinic sources. A midrash marvels at the greatness of *sh'lom bayit* for the sake of which even God edited Sarah's words when he relayed them to Abraham. (Sarah had expressed surprise at the news that they would have a child, given that she and Abraham were so old. God tactfully omitted Sarah's reference to her husband's age when he spoke to him.)

In the traditional Jewish world, *sh'lom bayit* is a project to be continuously worked on, not something to be taken for granted. There are classes and books full of good advice: compliment, praise or thank your spouse x times per day; don't contradict one another in public; talk things through but also push your powers of acceptance to the limit; don't make an issue of every annoying little difference of character, preference and habit; be nice to the in-laws, but don't expect very much of them, etc. These are things which may be blindingly obvious to old-timers but can save the marriage of young couples starting out.

shevah berakhot

Shevah berakhot are the mini-wedding parties that are made for Jewish couples during the week after their wedding. The traditional custom is not to jump on a plane to the Seychelles right away, but to celebrate with friends and family for a few days first. They are so called because of the seven marriage blessings which are said at grace after the meal during the week following the wedding, when a *minyan* is present.

These blessings, which are also part of the marriage ceremony, celebrate the love and joy of the new couple.

They look back to the joy of Adam and Eve in Eden, and forward to the rebuilding and rejoicing of Zion and Jerusalem. In this way, the blessings tell us that every new Jewish couple is an important link in the unbroken chain stretching from Eden to the future redemption of the Jewish people and the world.

Rabbi Aryeh Kaplan explains that one reason for having seven blessings, recited over seven days, is that each marriage has the potential for the creation of new life, and so is a re-enactment of the seven days of Creation.

The *shevah berakot* are only said during the marriage week when new faces who weren't at the wedding are present. This renews the joy of the celebration and allows you to invite guests for whom you didn't have room at the wedding. On Shabbat, you don't need to have new guests to say the *shevah berakot*. Shabbat itself is thought of as a new presence.

shiddukh

Jews don't do arranged marriages. Jewish law forbids a couple who have never met each other to marry. We do, however, have *shiddukhim*.

This is when you decide that your husband's business partner's daughter really ought to go out with your extremely eligible, inexplicably unmarried nephew. If the couple agree, then they meet ('go on a *shiddukh*'), and take it from there.

In more Orthodox circles, the couple may meet in a

very public place, such as a hotel lobby or an airport. They carry on meeting until they decide either to break up or get engaged. If they break up, they sometimes do so via their intermediary to avoid some of the attendant hurt and embarrassment.

This can be an intense system, but it has many advantages. When two people are brought together by a third who knows them both, they're likely to be in the right ball-park of compatibility. (Not always though. I once went went on a *shiddukh* which lasted eight minutes before we parted amicably, both wondering what our *shadchan* (matchmaker) had been thinking.)

In the Orthodox communities, where you date to find a mate, this saves a lot of time, frustration and potential heartbreak. It also involves your friends and family in seeking your life partner. Sometimes they can seem interfering, but in a world where finding a spouse can be a lonely, desperate business, this sort of communal support is often very welcome.

Making a *shiddukh*, bringing together two people who find love, happiness and create a new family together, is an enormous *mitzvah*. There's even a tradition which says that if you make three successful *shiddukhim*, you guarantee your place in the world to come.

simchah

Simchah translates fairly accurately into Anglo-Jewish as 'a catered dinner for 300 people with monogrammed invitations, a videographer and an 11-piece band'. Too many might be a cause for sympathy, as in 'poor woman, she's made three *simchahs* this year already'.

As we have seen with other words, the contemporary usage has strayed somewhat from the traditional meaning. *Simchah* means 'joy' or 'rejoicing'. Bar mitzvahs, weddings and other occasions for parties are certainly *simchahs* in that sense.

The menu is far from irrelevant to *simchah*, even in the Talmud. The *simchah* of *yomtov* – festivals – is said to be incomplete without meat and wine (Pesachim 109a). *Simchah* is a whole-body experience, encompassing the physical senses as well as the spiritual.

However, *simchah* is not just for special occasions; it's also the joy of everyday life. 'Serve God in *simchah*', says Psalm 100.

Simchah shel mitzvah, the joy of doing a *mitzvah*, is the best attitude with which to approach any good deed, including prayer (Talmud, Berachot, 31a).

Rebbe Nachman of Bratzlav reversed the idea of *simchah shel mitzvah*, with his advice that 'it's a big *mitzvah* to be *b'simchah*, joyful, all the time'.

Simchah, as Rav Kook defines it, is the emotion which naturally wells up in an upright soul knowing the goodness of the path it is on.

11

Redst du Yeshivish?

The growing phenomenon of kids taking a year or more after school for intensive Talmud study in a yeshivah has introduced yeshivish into mainstream English.

The world's foremost authority on 'Yeshivish', Chaim Weiser, author of Frumspeak: The First Dictionary of Yeshivish, *finds its roots in the perennnial Jewish drive to reshape the vernacular around them as a vehicle for holiness. Yeshivish is an amalgam of English, Yiddish and Aramaic adapted for the needs of Talmud study and yeshivah life. Finding the most direct expression for transmitting Torah trumps the Yeshivish-speaker's interest in linguistic purity. As Weiser puts it, 'knowing what the* nafka minah *is overrides any concern about what an English speaker should call it'.[1]* Nafka minah *is anyway far more economical than 'practical*

---

[1] Chaim Weiser, *Frumspeak: The First Dictionary of Yeshivish* (Northvale, 1995).

*or legal difference arising from a theoretical distinction',
which is my best shot at a translation.*

*A fascinating aspect of Yeshivish is how readily it transfers
words for abstruse Talmudic concepts into mundane contexts.
A recent yeshivah returnee might say at the dinner table,
'Coke or Pepsi? Who cares? What's the* nafka minah*?' This
reflects the power of Talmudic thinking to shape a whole
worldview.*

*Weiser attempts to demonstrate the versatility of Yeshivish
by translating certain passages from world literature into
Yeshivish, including Mark Anthony's funeral oration from
Julius Caesar, beginning* 'Raboisai, Roman oilam, hei-
mishe chevra, herr zich ain ...' *His stirring rendition of the
Gettysburg Address opens* 'Be'erech a yoivel *and a half ago,
the* meyasdim shtelled avek *on this* makom ...' *However,
Weiser admits that the lack of any original yeshivish literature
challenges the legitimacy of counting it as a viable language.*

ba'al teshuvah

A *ba'al teshuvah* is someone who has chosen to live a
more religious Jewish life. BTs for short, they are often
contrasted with FFBs (*frum* from birth), people who were
brought up religious. Though existing in traditional
Jewish literature for centuries, the word has become
widespread over the past 40 years with the striking return
to religious observance that has taken place over that time.
It can be used as an adjective, *ba'al teshuvah-ish*, meaning
behaviour characteristic of *ba'alei teshuvah*, (i.e. great zeal

for religious observance combined with a certain lack of the knowledge that underpins it).

The phrase may seem to be a misnomer. *Ba'al* means owner or master, and *teshuvah* which is often translated as 'repentance', really means 'return', from the verb *lashuv*. This sounds as if the *ba'al teshuvah* is going back to somewhere he was before, whereas most were never previously observant. Mystics such as Rabbi Abraham Isaac Kook explain that the path of *teshuvah* is a journey towards the divine source of all existence from which everything emanates. In this sense it is a return.

In some parts of the observant world, *ba'alei teshuvah* are of somewhat lower standing than those fortunate enough to grow up religious. This distinction is not supported by the majority of traditional sources of which I am aware. The Talmud (Berakhot 34b) writes that 'even the completely righteous cannot stand in the place of *ba'alei teshuvah*'. Commentators explain that one who has made the immense spiritual effort required to change his or her life has, by the power of that choice achieved more than one who was religious all along.

daled amot

Daled amot translates most accurately as 'personal space'. Using it in a sentence, one might say, 'Whether you choose to put on deodorant is your own business, as long as you stay out of my *daled amot*'.

A secondary sense of the phrase is an area of expertise,

as in 'Don't ask me about quantum physics, that's outside my *daled amot*'.

Daled amot measures about six feet: *daled* is the Hebrew letter corresponding to the number 4, and an *amah* is the biblical measure of a cubit, the distance from your elbow to your middle fingertip (roughly a foot and a half for most people.) In Jewish law, *daled amot* is a person's private domain.

Among the ramifications of this definition are that carrying an object a distance of more than four *amot* in a public domain on Shabbat violates a biblical prohibition; and that a man should not walk more than four *amot* with his head uncovered.

The Babylonian sage Ulla poignantly declared, 'Since the day the Temple was destroyed, all that remains for the Holy One, Blessed Be He, in His world are the four *amot* of *halakhah*' (Talmud, Berachot 8a). The sense seems to be that since the site of God's permanent dwelling in Jerusalem was erased, God is present in the private sphere within which we act according to his will.

Rabbi A.J. Heschel notes that this is hardly a jubilant statement expressing an ideal. We work and pray for the time when God's presence will return to our communal and national lives, and beyond.

davka

Davka is a word most Jews understand without necessarily being able to define it. This is probably to do with the long, strange journey which the word has taken from its original roots.

As used today, *davka* means something like 'just to annoy' (similar to *auftzuluchis*), or sometimes, 'in his own inimitable way'. As in 'She, *davka*, only wears green', or 'They drive on Shabbat, *davka*'; or sometimes even, 'He'd be a nice guy if he wasn't so *davka*'.

It's fascinating to trace how *davka* comes to bear this variety of meanings. Its root is the Aramaic verb *duch*, which means 'to grind up fine', or 'to turn into powder'. From this it is used in the Talmud to mean 'to examine something closely, carefully', or 'punctiliously'.

For example *lo duk* means 'He did not express himself precisely'. A *diyuk* is an inference derived from a close reading. Based on this, the word *davka* is used in the Talmud to mean 'precisely', 'exclusively' or 'only'. So, saying that matzah can be made *davka* from five types of grain means from those five and only those five.

Now we can see how a word meaning 'precisely this way and no other way' comes to be used of behaviour which is inimitable or exactly calibrated to annoy.

derech eretz

In contemporary Jewish parlance, *derech eretz* (literally 'the way of the land') means something like good manners or the done thing. If there's no other firm reason for disapproving of something, you might say, 'It's just not *derech eretz*.'

The traditional meanings of *derech eretz* encompass this but are also much broader. *Derech eretz* covers the basic norms of decent human behaviour which the Torah teaches, but which also in a sense precede Torah in forming the human personality: hence the maxim, '*Derech eretz* comes before Torah'.

The requirements of *derech eretz* include speaking calmly and gently to people; eating sitting down like a human being, rather than while walking in the street, like an animal; dressing in clothes that are clean and presentable, but not gaudy or extravagant; walking naturally rather than pretentiously or affectedly, and generally behaving like a *mensch*.

In the famous passage from Pirkei Avot (Ethics of the Fathers, 2.2), 'Torah is good, along with *derech eretz*', the phrase has a particular, specific meaning. Maimonides and the majority of commentators say it refers to doing productive work.

In the nineteenth century, '*derech eretz*' was given a new twist by Rabbi Samson Raphael Hirsch (1808–88), the German founder of modern or neo-Orthodoxy. He made 'Torah with *derech eretz*' the rallying cry of his movement, and understood it to mean the synthesis of Torah with all that is best in the surrounding culture.

gematria

Gematria is a Greek word that has entered Hebrew and refers to numerical interpretation of Hebrew words and letters.

Gematria has ancient roots in Jewish hermeneutics. It is mentioned in the 'Baraita of thirty-two rules', a compendium of techniques of biblical interpretation. In common with most of these rules, *gematria* was licensed only for *aggadic*, i.e. literary or homiletic interpretion, but not for the purposes of drawing halakhic, legal conclusions. Talmud Sukkah, 28a includes *gematria* in a long list of areas of Jewish study that Rabbi Yohanan Ben Zakkai mastered. The use of *gematria* multiplied in the writings of the Kabbalists, though Jewish thinkers including Nachmanides periodically warned against its excessive employment.

There are dozens of methods of *gematria*. The best-known involves assigning a numerical score to each letter of the Hebrew alphabet and then summing the total value of a word. So, for example, the word *ehad*, meaning 'one' has a *gematria* of 13 (*aleph*=1; *het*=8; *dalet*=4). Practitioners of *gematria* believe that the numerical value of a word reveals insights about its meaning, and its relationship to other words with the same, or similar *gematria*. They would think it no coincidence that the word *ahavah*, meaning 'love', like *ehad*, also has a *gematria* of 13 (*aleph*=1, *heh*=5, *vet*=2, *heh*=5). Love overcomes separateness and engenders oneness.

gushpanka

Gushpanka means *hechsher*, an 'imprimatur' or 'seal of approval', especially one coming from an authority figure whose endorsement is highly valued. You might speak of Rabbi X 'giving the *gushpanka*' to a book or a food product.

Because the word sounds inherently funny to British ears, *gushpanka* is also used ironically. Rabbi X might then be giving his *gushpanka* to something that does not in fact require rabbinical approval, such as a political party or a football team.

One might assume that *gushpanka*, like other faintly humorous-sounding Jewish words, is Yiddish in origin, but in fact it is Aramaic and appears several times in the Talmud, where it means 'signet' or 'seal'.

Berakhot 6a advises that in order to protect a certain precious dust from demons, one should seal it in an iron tube with an iron *gushpanka*. Gittin 57a tells of a Roman emperor who lit so many torches in his palace that the image engraved on his *gushpanka* was visible a mile away.

The ultimate origin of *gushpanka* is disputed. Jastrow's *Talmudic Dictionary* suggests that it is a running together of two words, *gush* meaning 'block,' and *panka* meaning 'freeman' or 'aristocrat' – the type of person who would have his own personal seal.

Rabbi Steinsaltz's translation of the Talmud maintains that the word is from the Persian *angustpanak*, meaning 'signet ring'. The letter *tav* was dropped when the word entered Aramaic because of the rarity of three consecutive closed consonants (*itzurim*) in Semitic languages.

halavai

Halavai, or *v'lavai* is a Talmudic expression used colloquially in *frum* circles – and by secular Israelis – to mean 'if only' or 'would that it were so'. One might say it feelingly as in '*Halavai*, that he should meet a nice Jewish girl'; or wistfully as in '*Halavai*, that I could spend more time learning Torah'; or ironically, as in '*Halavai*, that we should all be so clever.'

Halavai comes from the word *lu* (spelled *lamed vav*) meaning 'may it be so'. (Remember the campfire song by Naomi Shemer, *Lu Yehi* ?)

Lu first appears in the Bible when God promises Abraham that his wife Sarah will bear him a son, and an incredulous Abraham can only reply, '*Lu Yishmael yihyeh l'fanecha*' ('Would that Yishmael [Abraham's son by Hagar] should live before you') (Genesis 17.18).

The most poignant *v'lavai* in the Talmud occurs in Berachot 28b. Rabbi Yochanan Ben Zakkai is on his death-bed. His students ask him to bless them. He responds: 'May it be His will that the fear of heaven should be upon you like the fear of flesh and blood.'

The students are not impressed. 'Only that much?' they ask. (Surely a respectable blessing would be for the fear of heaven far to surpass their fear of human beings?) '*V'lavai* that it was that much,' answers the rabbi. 'For know that when a person sins, he says "let no man see me." '

Would that we cared as much about what God thinks

127

as about what other people think, is Rabbi Yochanan Ben Zakkai's blessing to his students.

hashgachah

You might hear someone raving about a new kosher restaurant, only to be confronted by the question, 'But what's the *hashgachah*?' – meaning, which kashrut authority is supervising and certifying the establishment? (Why there may be multiple kashrut authorities, even in the same city, is a good question beyond the scope of this article to answer.)

The on-site supervisor responsible for the kashrut in the restaurant is called the *mashgiach*. Sometimes people wonder what *mashgichim* do all day, but having served as one for six weeks in a well-known Golders Green restaurant, I can assure you that it's a demanding and responsible post.

Mashgiach (which comes from the Hebrew verb meaning to consider or take care of) is also the name for the rabbi in a school or yeshivah who is a counsellor and adviser responsible for the moral and spiritual development of the students. This position was an innovation of the nineteenth-century Musar movement of Rabbi Israel Salanter, which focused on refining the character and ethical behaviour of the students as much as on their intellectual attainments.

Hashgachah is also the word for God's providential attention to the world. Medieval Jewish philosophers argued over whether God exercised providence over individuals (*hashgachah pratit*) or over peoples (*hashgachah klalit*). A religious Jew will often attribute a fortuitous coincidence to *hashgachah*. As the Bible puts it, God looks upon (*mashgiach*) all the people of the world (Psalm 33.14).

hava amina

Hava amina is a common Talmudic phrase. People who have studied in yeshivah tend to find that it's a very handy expression in everyday life too.

Hava amina means 'what I would have said' in Aramaic, the language of Jews in Babylon at the time of the Talmud. Here's how it's used: the Mishnah or Talmud makes a statement about the world, such as 'All Israel has a place in the World to Come' (Talmud Sanhedrin, 90a). Then you want to know what was the Talmud's *hava amina*; that is, what would you have thought or said if the Talmud had not made this statement. (In this case, you might perhaps have thought that someone who denies the existence of the World to Come has no place in it.) The *hava amina* is the alternative reality which the actual statement made comes to contradict.

In Talmudic thinking, if there is no plausible *hava amina*, then the statement made is nonsensical or empty. If your mother-in law exclaims 'I'm not perfect', you might justifiably ask yourself, what was her *hava amina*?

That she is perfect? If that's not a sensible presumption, then 'I'm not perfect' isn't a meaningful statement. Or one might say 'I didn't even have a *hava amina* to vote Labour', meaning that the possibility was so outlandish as not to deserve any serious consideration. It is characteristic of the Talmud to assume that every biblical or Mishnaic statement which it analyses has a point. There must be a *hava amina*, or else the statement is superfluous.

It is also characteristic of Talmudic thinking that we want to understand the *hava amina* as deeply as possible. Although it is the opposite of what we conclude, we only really understand the conclusion when we fully grasp the possibility which it excludes.

havruta

Study with a *havruta*, or partner, is a hallmark of traditional Jewish learning. Together you break your heads on the texts. Two minds applied to a problem are almost always better than one. Each checks and corrects the misconceptions of the other, questioning and sharpening the other's ideas, while the necessity of articulating one's thoughts to another person brings greater clarity than learning alone. Indeed, the Talmud goes so far as to say that one who learns Torah alone becomes stupid! (Berakhot 63a.)

Havruta comes from the Hebrew word meaning, simply, 'friend'. Pirkei Avot (Ethics of the Fathers) states the fundamental importance of companionship in Jewish learning (and in general): 'Make for yourself a teacher, find yourself a friend, and judge every person favourably'. Commentators explain the final, apparently unrelated, clause as being an essential requirement for achieving the first two. Being endlessly judgemental and critical makes it very hard to commit to, (and keep) either friends or teachers.

There are numerous statements in the sources that stress the essential sociability of study. The unbearability of life without scholarly companionship is poignantly expressed about Honi the Circle-maker, 'Either *havruta* or *mituta*', 'either friendship or death' (Taanit 23a).

Some suggest that the quality of relationship between the *havrutas* is as important religiously as the content of what is studied. 'When two scholars of Torah listen to one another, God hears their voices', says the Talmud (Shabbat 63a).

hiddush

Ein beit midrash bli hiddush: there is no house of study without innovation, runs a popular saying. Original interpretation is essential to the process of traditional Jewish study.

The proudest achievement of a yeshivah student is to arrive at a *hiddush*, a new addition to the accumulated knowledge of the generations. Rabbis publish their most treasured insights in books of *hiddushim*, new writings which present original twists of argument and interpretation.

131

It may seem surprising that yeshivah study, which places such weight on traditional authority, should also value *hiddush*, which is a noun-form of *hadash* meaning, simply, 'new'.

Rabbi Joseph Soloveitchik (1903–93) distinguishes between *hiddush* (innovation) within a tradition, and *shinui* (change) which represents a sharp break from tradition. In Rabbi Soloveitchik's view, *hiddush* is an aspect of *imitatio Dei* (imitation of God). Through it we become creative partners with God in the unfolding of the Torah's meanings. On the other hand, *shinui*, which is not deeply rooted in traditional knowledge, risks becoming subjective and arbitrary.

Hiddush is so common a word among speakers of Yeshivish (the dialect of English spoken by those who have spent a long time in yeshivah) that it has entered everyday use. In this context, it means something like a surprising discovery or invention, as in 'It's a *hiddush* to me that the *Jewish Chronicle* has a column on Jewish words'.

humrah

A *humrah* is a voluntarily assumed restriction more stringent than what is required by Jewish law. For example, drinking only *chalav Yisrael*, supervised milk, is a *humrah* according to most authorities. In a country like Britain, with high standards of food regulation, the chances of milk being tampered with are negligible.

Humrah comes from the word *hamur*, meaning heavy,

grave or serious. Keeping *humrahs* can be an admirable part of saintly religious behaviour. However, there are rabbinic sources that caution against adopting them. 'Are the Torah's prohibitions not enough to you, that you have come to create new prohibitions for yourself?' asks the Jerusalem Talmud (Nedarim 9.1).

In his classical ethical work, *Mesillat Yesharim* (The Path of the Just), Rabbi Moshe Chaim Luzzatto advocates stringency beyond what the Torah demands only after one has achieved scrupulous observance of all that is required – a lifetime's work for most people.

Furthermore, *humrah* is meant to be a level of religious observance that exceptional individuals may take upon themselves, rather than one which is adopted by a whole community as if it is a norm. And one may adopt *humrahs* in *tzedakah*, giving charity, or *lashon hara*, harmful gossip, just as much as in the areas of kashrut and Shabbat.

mehadrin

Mehadrin is often used to mean 'extremely kosher', but this isn't quite right. Applied to fulfilling *mitzvot*, *mehadrin* means 'beautiful', or 'distinguished'. As Rabbi Yehudah Henkin points out, a wedding or bar mitzvah may be under *mehadrin* kashrut supervision, but if it is gaudy, extravagant and conceived in a spirit of out-spending the Cohens, it is far from being a *mehadrin* fulfilment of the *mitzvah*.

Mehadrin derives from *hadar* which means 'to enclose' or 'go around'. From this it comes to mean a crown or adornment, from which we see how *mehadrin* refers to a manner of doing a *mitzvah* with special distinction.

Mehadrin is first used in this sense in the Talmud's discussion of lighting Hanukah candles (Shabbat 21b). The Talmud states that the standard way of fulfilling the *mitzvah* is for each family to light one candle on each night of the holiday. The *mehadrin* manner is for every member of the family to light one candle each night. The *mehadrin min hamehadrin* (i.e. outstandingly punctilious way) is (according to the house of Hillel) for each member of the household to light one candle on the first night, two on the second, etc. (Some opinions hold that the *mehadrin min hamehadrin* level is attained by lighting one set of ascending numbers of candles for the whole home.)

This example shows us how *mehadrin* observance is partially a function of what is socially considered to be such. The practice of filling the house with light so that the Talmud was '*mehadrin min hamehadrin*' has become the norm in every Jewish home where the miracles of Hanukah are celebrated.

Mishnah

A paradox of Judaism is that it contains libraries of written books recording and elaborating the Oral Law, Torah Sheba'al Peh. But oral means 'not written'. This paradox dates back to the Mishnah, the first layer of Oral

Law to be codified in written form, during the second century CE. Before the Mishnah, the Torah Sheba'al Peh, originating at Sinai, was transmitted and developed orally from teacher to student.

However, in the generations following the destruction of the Temple when many sages were killed and many more were scattered, Rabbi Yehudah Hanasi took it upon himself to write down the oral discussions in the form of the Mishnah, reasoning that otherwise the Oral Law could be lost altogether.

The word *mishnah* means teaching. It appears in the Shema, *v'shinantam l'vanecha*, 'You shall teach them to your children'. It comes from the word *shanah*, meaning repetition – the most basic mode of teaching. The sages of the Mishnah are known as *tana'im*, meaning teachers in Aramaic. *Shanah* also means year, the eternally repeating cycle of time.

There is an ancient tradition to study Mishnah at a *shivah* house. One reason for this is that the word *mishnah* comprises the same letters (*mem*, *shin*, *nun*, *heh*) as the word *neshamah*, soul. Studying Mishnah is a way of honouring the departed soul.

Moshiach

Moshiach, meaning 'Messiah' is a word that you're most likely to have heard in two songs often played at weddings, 'We want *Moshiach* now!' and '*Moshiach*, *Moshiach*, *Moshiach*!' (The band who played at our wedding have a strict policy of performing only on the clear prior understanding that they will not have to play these songs – for aesthetic rather than theological reasons.)

Although mystical views of the *Moshiach* exist in Jewish tradition, the mainstream view is rationalistic. The Messiah doesn't have to perform signs, wonders or miracles. According to Maimonides (Laws of Kings 11.4), the *Moshiach* will be someone who studies Torah, keeps the *mitzvot*, becomes a ruler over Israel bringing the people back to observe Judaism, fights the 'wars of God', rebuilds the Temple, gathers in the scattered Jewish exiles, inspires the whole world to recognize the one God, and initiates an era of universal peace – a demanding though fairly transparent set of criteria.

The Messianic age for which we yearn is seen as a time of justice and peace, without hunger, war, envy or competition, when all will be free to pursue wisdom and knowledge of God.

Over the past 2,000 years a series of Jews, including Jesus and Shabbetai Zevi, have either claimed to be the *Moshiach* or have had followers claim it on their behalf. However, none of them has yet fulfilled Maimonides' criteria, and so their messianic claims have not been accepted by most of the Jewish people.

payos

Payos, or *payot* are part of the identifiable regalia of

Haredi Jews. Men and boys make *payot* by growing their side-locks long and either leaving them hanging in ringlets or curling and tucking them behind their ears.

Growing *payos* is an interpretation of the command-ment in Leviticus 19.27: 'You shall not round the corners (*payot*) of your heads, nor shall you destroy the corners of your beards'. The commentators explain that idolators characteristically shaved in those places. We do not like to follow fashions whose origins were idolatrous. The *halakhah* restricts the prohibition to shaving with a naked blade that touches the skin (see Maimonides, Laws of Idolatry, 12.6). Most types of electric shaver do not; this is why one can find religiously observant Jewish men without beards. However, even they avoid shaving their sideburns above the cheekbone in deference to this commandment.

The other issue of *payos* in Jewish law is the commandment in the same chapter of the Torah, 'Do not wholly reap the corners (*payot*) of your fields' (Leviticus 19.9). Farmers may not harvest the corners of their fields (how much of the corner is left undefined by the Torah: see Mishnah Peah, 1.1), but must leave them for the poor to come and glean after them.

peshat

Peshat, means 'the plain, straightforward meaning' of something. It comes from the root of the word 'to straighten, stretch out, flay or strip'.

It is used colloquially, especially by people with a yeshivah background. For example, after hearing some convoluted story about how your sister's friend was stood up three times by the same guy, you can ask '*Nu*, what's *peshat*?' meaning, 'What's the real reason why he didn't turn up?'

As a slight variation, the exclamation '*peshitah*' means 'that's obvious', and is thus roughly equivalent to '*duh*' in American.

Peshat also refers to the school of biblical interpretation which focused on the plain meaning of the text rather than the midrashic elaborations. It arose in the eleventh and twelfth centuries, and was especially associated with Rashbam, Ibn Ezra and their students.

Nechama Leibowitz, the great twentieth-century Bible teacher, shows that *peshat* is not always literal but can sometimes be contextual. She points out that when the angels come and visit Abraham and ask, 'Where is Sarah your wife?' (Genesis 18.9), the *peshat* of their question is, 'Why isn't she here?'

Similarly, Leibowitz would explain: suppose I have a puncture and am trying to jack up my car when a well-meaning soul stops and enquires 'Do you have a puncture?' If I yell at him, 'Of course I do, you moron, what does it look like?' then I haven't understood the *peshat* of his question, which was 'Can I help?'

psik reisha

Psik reisha is a Talmudic expression meaning 'an inevitable consequence'. Its main application is to the laws of Shabbat. We'll need a little background to understand the concept.

A permitted action on Shabbat that may possibly lead to a forbidden consequence is permitted. (For example, it's OK to walk across grass on Shabbat, even though you might thereby inadvertently detach grass with your feet.) However, when the action will inevitably lead to a forbidden consequence, this is not so; the action is forbidden. This situation is called a *psik reisha*, which means 'cutting the head' in Aramaic. (*Reisha* is related to the Hebrew for head, *rosh*.)

The name comes from the Talmud's paradigmatic case of a *psik reisha* (Shabbat 103a). A man wants to cut off the head of a chicken in order to provide a diverting toy for his child. (This was in the days before Play Stations.) He has no intention of killing the chicken; to do so would be forbidden. (Slaughtering is one of the 39 categories of work that may not be done on Shabbat.) 'But can you cut the head off a chicken and the chicken won't die?' asks the Talmud incredulously. Of course it will. This is a clear example of an unintended consequence of an action that will inevitable transpire; hence the expression.

seichel

Seichel means wit or intelligence. In the expressions, 'use a bit of *seichel*', or 'pity they don't teach you *seichel* at that university of yours', it's roughly synonymous with nous, noddle or common sense. Modern Hebrew uses the expression *sechel hayashar* for common sense.

Seichel is derived from the word meaning to be bright or see clearly. In the Bible the wise or enlightened are known as *maskilim*, from the same root. The *maskilim* are said to shine like the sky (Daniel 12.3), and King David was described as *maskil* in all his ways.

In the late eighteenth century the Jewish strain of the European Enlightenment called themselves *maskilim*, and their movement the Haskalah. The early *maskilim* in Eastern Europe were religious Jews whose innovativeness consisted of reading secular literature and trying to revive Hebrew as a spoken and written language.

As the Haskalah moved westwards, it became especially associated with Moses Mendelssohn and his circle. Mendelssohn's contemporaries wrote in Hebrew, but the next generation of *maskilim* became cut off from Jewish sources and wrote in German. Many of them assimilated or converted to Christianity. Haskalah became irrelevant to the Jewish masses and disappointed the hopes vested in it for a renewal of Jewish life.

shiur

Shiur has two common uses. In the first, it means a class or lecture on any Torah subject. *Shiurim* may be about Talmud, the weekly *parashah*, Hasidism, mysticism or any other area rooted in traditional Jewish sources.

The word means literally 'a quantity, measure or amount', deriving from *sha'ar*, meaning gate, that is, an opening of a certain size. So *shiur* in this first meaning just means an amount or chunk of Torah.

The second meaning is more literal. In this sense a *shiur* is the precise amount or measurement of material that is necessary for defining whether a *mitzvah* has been done or a prohibition transgressed. So, there is a minimum *shiur* of matzah to be eaten in order to fulfil the *mitzvah* of eating matzah on Seder night, a *kazayit* (that is an olive's volume, though olives in the time of the Talmud seem to have been larger than those of today).

There is a minimum *shiur* of distance for violating the prohibition against carrying in the public domain on Shabbat (four cubits, about six feet), and minimum *shiurim* for the amount of a substance that we need to carry in order to have violated that prohibition. (These depend on the type of substance or object in question.)

Across the whole range of Jewish law, there are *shiurim* determining when and how we infuse the physical world with holiness through doing *mitzvot*.

shteig

To *shteig* is yeshivah-speak for learning Torah. You might point admiringly to a friend immersed in study and say, 'Look at him, *shteiging* away, *mamash shtark* [truly devotedly], in his corner as usual'.

Shteig is Yiddish, derived from the German meaning to

rise or ascend. It comes to refer to studying Torah as this is the main Jewish path to spiritual ascent. One could say, 'Just remember, you're *shteiging* with every moment of learning'.

Rabbi Yitzchak Hutner (1908–84) points out an anomaly in this use of *shteig*, which seems to pervade Yiddish. Rabbi Hutner notes that the Talmudic rabbis, wherever possible, applied different words to the domains of the holy and the secular, even when the word ostensibly means the same. (He gives the example of the two words, *haramah* and *hagba'ah*, which both mean to raise up: the former refers to spiritual elevation, the latter to the physical acquisition of something.)

'We', he writes (meaning Yiddish-speakers) 'have no such distinction.' *Shteig* means to rise in both areas. In a secular sense, it means to accumulate wealth and possessions; in the realm of spirituality, it is to grow in wisdom. The applications are very different but it's the same word.

It seems to be characteristic of Yiddish in general that the holy and profane meet in its expressions, evoking the Jewish world of Eastern Europe, where the spiritual and the everyday were so intertwined.

siyyum

Siyyum means conclusion or finishing (deriving from the verb *som*, meaning to place, which comes to mean a marker). The *siyyum ha'shas* is the culmination of the seven-and-a-half year *daf yomi* cycle, when tens of thousands of people round the world celebrate the completion of the Babylonian Talmud.

It's common to hold a *siyyum* also to mark more modest achievements in Jewish learning. People will often open a bottle of schnapps and a box of biscuits after *shul* on a weekday morning to celebrate completing a tractate of Talmud.

There's widespread tradition of holding a *siyyum* after *shul* on the morning of the fast of the first-born, immediately before Pesach. The rationale is that first-borns who would otherwise have had to fast may eat at the *siyyum*, in order to participate in the Seudat *mitzvah*, the meal that celebrates a significant religious achieve-ment. Having broken their fast at the *siyyum*, they are allowed to carry on eating throughout the day.

I've heard this custom described as a cop-out. People ask, why should you get out of fasting because you hear someone read the last few lines of a Talmudic tractate and eat a biscuit? I suspect that only someone who hasn't felt the joy of completing a volume of the Talmud could raise this objection. The investment of intense mental and spiritual effort that yields a measure of mastery over an area of Torah and an appreciation of its intricate interwoven themes is enough cause for celebration, whether the achievement is yours or your friend's.

stam

Stam is a word which has enjoyed a long and varied career from the Bible to modern Hebrew.

In the Tanakh it means 'stop up', usually referring to the flow of waters. For example, *satam* is used to describe the vandalism that the Philistines inflict on the wells that Abraham dug (Genesis 26.15).

In Mishnaic Hebrew, *stam* means 'closed', in the sense of concealed or not explicitly stated. A *stam mishnah* is one which is not attributed to any particular teacher. A *parsha setuma*, or closed *parsha* in the Torah is one which is separated from the previous *parsha* by a space in the middle of the line as opposed to a *parsha petuha*, an open *parsha*, which has a space at the beginning of the line. The *parsha* of Vayehi is written *setuma*, according to Rashi (in Genesis 49.1) to hint to us that in Egypt, at the end of his life, Jacob's insight was stopped up just as he was about to reveal the secrets of the End of Days to his sons.

In Yiddish, *stam* means 'simply, or for no reason'. To speak *stam azoi* in Yiddish means to talk randomly, without logic. In Israeli playgrounds, *stam*! means 'I was just kidding', i.e. there was no reason for what I said.

Stam is also the source for the Yiddish *stumm*, as in 'keep *stumm*', meaning keep quiet, don't tell anyone. *Stumm* is etymologically unrelated to *stam*, but comes from the German for dumb, mute or stupid.

Talmud

'Talmud' means learning or teaching, derived from *lamed*, which means to learn. The Talmud is arguably the most important Jewish book (or set of books – the standard edition comes in 20 volumes).

It is a record of discussions and debates which took place over hundreds of years, and which were committed to writing around the year 600 CE. Its source is the oral Torah, the core of which was received at the same time as the written Torah. The oral Torah developed and expanded through interpretation, logical derivation and case-law until it was written down around the year 200 CE as the Mishnah. The ensuing 400 years of discussion about the Mishnah is called the Gemara. The Mishnah and Gemara together comprise the Talmud.

The subject matter of the Talmud is all-encompassing. The legal parts (called *halakhah*) cover agriculture, business, Shabbat and festivals, family law and more. The non-legal parts (*aggadah*) include biblical interpretation, philosophical reflection, mysticism, fantastic stories, medical remedies, recipes, etc.

The Talmud argues about the weightiest questions imaginable (Would it have been better for humans to be created, or not? What should two men in the desert with only enough water for one do?), as well as more everyday issues.

Study of Talmud has been central to Jewish life and continuity for 1,400 years. It's impossible to convey in a few words the fascination of this text which still entrances the most brilliant minds to this day. Try it for yourself and find out.

yeshivish

Yeshivish is an adjective of broad scope that may refer to the values, style, manners or language of the *yeshivot*, the institutions of Talmud study that are today the powerhouses of the Orthodox Jewish world. In colloquial use one might say that Mickey Mouse socks are not a very yeshivish article of clothing, or that you'd prefer to move to Edgware as it's a more yeshivish area than Mill Hill.

Academies of Torah study, known as *yeshivot*, have existed for at least 2,000 years. The word derives from *yoshev*, meaning to sit, which is a basic precondition for learning anything. Today you can still say, 'After sitting in yeshivah for twelve years, he is a big *talmid hakham* [Torah scholar]'.

For most of Jewish history, *yeshivot* served to produce the elite of rabbinical leadership. After around 1800, the great Lithuanian *yeshivot* aspired to educate a broader swathe of the Jewish public, and since the Second World War, the *yeshivot* of Israel and the United States have become the principal engine for the renewal of Orthodox life in the wake of the Shoah. This sweeping role accounts for the profound influence of yeshivah mores on the Orthodox community at large.

Graduates of English or American *yeshivot* speak a dialect that is closely related to English, but with an admixture of Yiddish, Aramaic, Hebrew and technical terms from Talmud study that can render it almost incomprehensible to outsiders. Chaim Weiser, an American linguist, has defined Yeshivish as a separate language, and compiled its first-ever dictionary, *Frumspeak* (see Introduction to this chapter).

zekhus

Zekhut (or *zekhus* in Ashkenazi pronunciation) means something between an advantage, a privilege or a reward. Often it is an advantage or honour that is felt to be a reward. You might say, 'It's a *zekhus* for me to look after you', or 'It was a *zekhus* to meet the Lubavitcher Rebbe', or 'He's so football-mad, he feels that the biggest *zekhus* of his life was to be at the 1966 World Cup Final'.

Zekhut derives from the word *zach*, meaning pure or clear. (The Torah speaks of *shemen zayit zach*, pure olive oil.) From there it came to mean to be acquitted or to be right, particularly in a legal case, and then to mean merit or worthiness more generally.

People speak of *zechuyot* as the accumulated power of good deeds. In the weeks leading up to Rosh Hashanah and Yom Kippur, we try to earn all the extra *zekhuyot* we can.

Maimonides writes, in his Laws of Teshuvah (3.4), that we should act as if we knew that our *zekhuyot* and *avonot*, sins, were balanced exactly equally. He stresses, though, that we have no idea how, quantitatively, different good and bad actions are weighed: only God knows.

Moreover, we should imagine the world to be in the same state of equilibrium between good and evil. At any moment then, one good action could tip the balance towards good for us and for the whole world.

12

The World of Kabbalah

Kabbalah is ancient Jewish wisdom about how spiritual energy creates and directs the universe. It also describes how the practice of Torah, mitzvot and good deeds affects these energies and so helps sustain the world. Works on Kabbalah fill libraries. Traditionally, Kabbalah was esoteric, the province of men who devoted lifetimes to study and spiritual purification.

The Hasidic spiritual revival of the eighteenth century aimed at expanding the influence of Kabbalah by incorporating some of its ideas into the study and practice of ordinary Jews. This democratization of Kabbalah took a further big step forward in the 1960s. Seeing the spread of spiritual and mystical consciousness in the West based on Eastern sources, Jewish leaders such as Rabbi Menachem Schneerson, the Lubavitcher Rebbe, advocated teaching some kabbalistic ideas to even the most assimilated Jews. In the climate of the times, he viewed Kabbalah as the dimension of Judaism most likely to engage disaffected Jews.

The Kabbalah craze of recent years has extended

awareness, if not knowledge, of Kabbalah across the globe. Millions saw Madonna wearing tefillin and bearing pseudo-Kabbalistic tattoos in an MTV video. Kabbalah is main-stream. I've therefore included this section on the most commonly used Kabbalistic words, the names of the ten sefirot *drawing mainly on Rabbi Aryeh Kaplan's authoritative book,* Inner Space.[1]

(Note: Instead of listing the sefirot *alphabetically, I have observed their traditional Kabbalistic order.)*

sefirot

Sefirot is an important kabbalistic term of art denoting the basic modes of God's creative power. Through the ten *sefirot*, God is said to interact with and influence creation.

The *sefirot* are not God, but they do allow us to speak of God's immanence in the world: what God does, rather than what God is, of which we can say nothing.

In English, the ten *sefirot* are Crown, Wisdom, Understanding, Love, Restraint, Beauty, Dominance, Empathy, Foundation and Kingship. In the kabbalistic system, each of these is associated with a particular part of the human body. Neither the spiritual characteristic nor the corresponding physical limb should be understood as being literally attributed to God. Rather, they are

---

[1] Aryeh Kaplan, *Inner Space* (New York, 1990). Rabbi Kaplan is one of the greatest modern popularizers of Kabbalah.

profound metaphors through which the kabbalists speak of God's powers.

The term *sefirah* itself is related to the Hebrew *saper*, meaning 'to express' or 'communicate'; to *sapir*, 'sapphire', 'brilliance' or 'radiance'; and also to *safar*, meaning 'number'.

The etymologies express the kabbalists' sense that the *sefirot* communicate, transmit and filter God's light to the world.

With the Madonna-ization of popular Kabbalah, the names of the *sefirot* are entering the everyday language of spiritual self-help, as in 'He really needs to rebalance his *hesed* and *gevurah* sides', or 'I'm trying to work on being more of a *hod* person'. But for the prevalence of these sorts of representations of kabbalistic concepts, it would be unacceptable to try to describe them in a simplistic way.

keter

Keter, or *keter elyon* meaning 'crown', is the first and highest of the ten Kabbalistic *sefirot* through which God's influence is channelled to the world. Words like 'first' and 'highest' need to be used with caution in this context. *Keter* is considered to be first in the sense of being closest to the divine source of emanation. In kabbalistic texts, the *sefirot* were represented diagramatically by an inverted tree, or by geometrical drawings of interconnected spheres. In these schema, *keter* was located at the top.

Keter corresponds to the characteristic of will. The primacy of *keter* testifies to the kabbalists' placing of will higher than any other faculty. God's will to create the world came 'before' the intellectual conception. (For the kabbalists, the divine will to create was motivated by a will to give, which was to find its fullest expression through human beings, the peak of creation.) The kabbalists differed from Jewish philosophers such as Maimonides in that they saw will rather than intellect as the highest human ability. It is by virtue of our ability to will and choose our actions freely that we are creatures in the image of God.

In the anthropomorphic picture of the *sefirot* as each corresponding to a part of the human body, *keter* occupies a slightly anomalous position. It is depicted as a point just above the human head. This represents the concept of will being prior to intellect in our process of thought, as well as in what makes us distinctively human.

binah

Binah is the third of the kabbalistic *sefirot*. Today it means 'intelligence' in modern Hebrew. For the kabbalists, *binah* comprises the analytic powers of the intellect.

In contrast to *chochmah*, the holistic intuitive mind, *binah* refers to the functions of logic and reasoning. Whereas *chochmah* is the initial inspired flash of a thought, *binah* is the subsequent thinking process through which we work out and develop the original idea.

In the kabbalistic map of the sefirot, *binah* is located on the left side of the head, corresponding as it does to what psychologists today call 'left-brain thinking'.

In the Talmud, *binah* is described as the faculty of 'understanding one thing from something dissimilar' (Sanhedrin 93b). Exodus 31.3 tells us that Bezalel was filled with wisdom, understanding (*binah*) and knowledge, and the medieval commentator Abraham Ibn Ezra points out that *binah* is related to the word *bein* meaning 'between.' So *binah* implies distance and separation. The nature of analytical thinking is to grasp the differences and distances between concepts.[2]

For the kabbalists, *binah* is associated with the feminine. As I noted above, *hokhmah*, the initial fertilizing seed of thought is linked to the masculine. *Binah* is the process through which this seed is gestated, nurtured and developed over a period of time until it reaches full fruition.

gevurah

Gevurah is the fifth *sefirah*. It is best translated as 'restraint' or 'limitation', although the literal meaning of *gevurah* is 'strength', deriving from '*gever*', meaning 'man'.

The connection between the literal meaning and the kabbalistic sense of *gevurah* as 'restraint' can be understood by reference to the saying from Pirkei Avot, the the Ethics of the Fathers (4.1): 'Who is strong [*gibor*]? The

---

[2]   See Rabbi Kaplan *Inner Space* (New York, 1990) for more on this.

one who restrains his inclination.' Spiritual strength lies in self-discipline.

Gevurah is the voluntary limitation of God's *hesed*, the powers of unlimited giving. A world created entirely through *hesed* would overwhelm us, leaving no room for choice or for separate identities. When *hesed* is moderated by *gevurah*, then it can be received by finite human beings.

Gevurah represents the second day of Creation, on which God made the firmament or skies, which set a limit to the expanse of Creation. (This needs to be understood metaphorically.) In the anthropomorphic map of the *sefirot*, *gevurah* is the left arm. The biblical figure who most embodied the characteristic of *gevurah* was Isaac. In consenting to be bound on the altar by his father, Isaac entirely restrained, indeed nullified, his own will before that of Abraham.

Gevurah also represents law, form or structure. Taken to extremes, it becomes cold, impersonal or even cruel. Set in the right balance with other characteristics, however, the ability to set limits and boundaries is an essential aspect of healthy living.

hesed

Hesed, meaning 'love', or 'kindness', is the fourth of the kabbalistic *sefirot*. It is God's power of unconditional giving which sustains Creation, and which we can emulate in our actions.

The Talmud writes that the only way in which we can meaningfully imitate God, who is in essence unknowable, is through deeds of loving-kindness: visiting the sick, clothing the naked, burying the dead, etc. (Sotah 14). Burying the dead is termed *hesed shel emet*, true *hesed* which one does without any hope of being repaid by the recipient.

Hesed is also the first of what are known as the seven lower *sefirot*. Each of those parallels one of the seven days of Creation. *Hesed* corresponds to the first day, which saw the creation of light. Rabbi Aryeh Kaplan points out that light, like pure *hesed*, is boundless and unrestrained.[3]

Each of the seven lower *sefirot* corresponds to a biblical personality who especially exemplified that trait. *Hesed* is represented by Abraham, who prepared food for travellers, went out to greet them, and whose tent was open towards all four directions. Abraham also gave himself over completely to pleading for the people of Sodom.

Undiluted *hesed* is not sustainable as a basis for Creation or as a principle by which to live. The kabbalists teach that the world would be overwhelmed by God's unrestrained *hesed* and that we would lose our identities if we tried to live in that way. *Hesed* needs to be moderated by the next *sefirah*: *gevurah*.

---

[3]   Ibid.

hokhmah

Hokhmah, the second of the ten kabbalistic *sefirot* means 'wisdom.' (*Hokhmah* has also entered colloquial language as a term for cleverness, often used ironically, as in 'Only a *chocham* like that could do something so stupid.')

In the kabbalistic scheme, *hokhmah* is one of the basic intellectual components with which God conceived and planned Creation. One source for this notion is the biblical verse, 'God founded the earth with wisdom [*hokhmah*] and established the heavens with *binah* [understanding]' (Proverbs 3.19).

Furthermore, Bezalel, the principal architect of the sanctuary is filled with '*hokhmah*, *binah* and *da'at*' (Exodus 31.3). The sanctuary is understood to be a microcosm of the world, therefore the same qualities are needed for its making.

Rabbi Arye Kaplan understands *hokhmah* as encompassing the basic axioms that define the world. A related idea is that *hokhmah* is the initial creative flash that begins the thought process and is subsequently worked out in analytical thinking. *Hokhmah* is similar to what psychologists describe as right-brain mental functioning – the holistic and intuitive activity of the mind. In this light, it is interesting that in their anthropomorphic map of the *sefirot*, the kabbalists located *hokhmah* on the right side of the head.

In kabbalistic archetypes, *hokhmah* is also identified with the male, in that it is the seed, the initial catalyst, that sets off the process of thought and creation.

tiferet

Tiferet, the sixth *sefirah*, means 'beauty'. It is beauty in the classical sense of harmonious balance, the proper blend of freedom and form, self-expression and self-discipline.

For the kabbalists, *tiferet* was specifically the balance of *hesed*, 'love' and *gevurah*, 'restraint'. *Tiferet* represents the mix of *hesed* and *gevurah* in God's interaction with the world. It corresponds to the third day of Creation, on which God established the boundaries between the overflowing seas and the firm dry land.

Plants were also created on the third day, with their combination of spontaneous growth, and clear boundaries between them and the rest of the world.

Jacob is the biblical character who best expressed *tiferet*. He is neither a pure altruist like Abraham nor a figure of self-subjugation like Isaac. Jacob grapples with the complexities of life: with Esau, his violent threatening brother, and with Laban, an exploitative employer.

He has to work out when it is right to give, and when he should hold back; when to overlook unfair treatment (for example, when Laban exchanges Leah for Rachel) and when to stand up for himself (when he finally leaves Laban after twenty years). Jacob strives to find equilibrium and so expresses the whole range of human emotions, from love to anger.

In relationships, *tiferet* is the difficult, though necessary, balance between giving of oneself to the point of surrendering our identity to the other person, and maintaining boundaries and a sense of one's own selfhood. *Tiferet* represents the successful integration of these contrasting modes of interacting with another person.

netzach

Netzach, 'dominance', is the seventh kabbalistic *sefirah*. Together with its complementary opposite, *hod*, 'empathy', it represents another important polarity in the way in which, according to the kabbalists, God influences the world.

Netzach is that way of being in a relationship which is self-assertive but, if taken to an extreme, overbearing or crushing. *Netzach* is derived from the word *menatzeach*, which means 'to conquer' or 'overcome', and is related to *l'netzach*, which means 'for eternity'. Self-assertion is necessary, but within limits. We must also know when to step back and leave space for the other.

The biblical character who most embodies *netzach* is Moses. He gave the Torah, the Divine Law, to the Israelites when they were in a position to exercise free choice about whether or not they would accept it.

The mystics teach that Moses' prophecy was received through the divine *sefirah* of *netzach*. Prophecy, the prophets tell us, is an experience beyond reason, in which the recipient's senses cease to function and the prophet feels utterly overwhelmed by God's presence and message.

Netzach is also the fourth of the lower *sefirot* and so

corresponds to the fourth day of Creation, on which God made the sun, the moon and the stars. Rabbi Aryeh Kaplan explains the connection: 'There was no reciprocity in the creation of the heavenly bodies. They were set in the heavens and made to follow eternal, unchangeable laws of planetary motion.'[4]

hod

Hod, the eighth kabbalistic *sefirah*, meaning 'empathy', is the opposite of *netzach*. Whereas *netzach* is the capacity for self-assertion, *hod* is the complementary power of submission or self-abnegation. *Hod* is related to *hoda'ah*, which connotes 'submission', 'acknowledgement' or 'thanks'.

When one makes space for someone else to act or express themselves in a relationship, by listening, or restraining oneself, one is exercising *hod*. Knowing how to mix *netzach* and *hod* in the right proportions is key to good relationships.

Aaron was the biblical archetype of *hod*. He 'loved peace and pursued peace' (Ethics of the Fathers), which required him to listen and to limit himself. It was this attribute of *hod* taken to excess that allowed Aaron to acquiesce in the sin of the Golden Calf. His submission to the will of the people was such that he was unable to stand up against the evil they initiated. Only Moses, the

---

[4] Ibid.

prototype of *netzach*, 'dominance', was able to put a stop to it.

In the kabbalistic map of the body, *netzach* and *hod* correspond to the right and left feet respectively (or according to some, the kidneys).

Rabbi Aryeh Kaplan explains that the humble activity of walking exemplifies *netzach* and *hod* in harmony. At any moment, one foot is active, raised and striding forward, while the other is passive, grounded and providing necessary balance. Only through our instinctive knowledge of which foot to move and which foot to keep still are we able to progress.[5]

yesod

Yesod, meaning 'foundation' is the penultimate kabbalistic *sefirah*. It is also known as *yesod olam* (foundation of the world) or *tzaddik*, righteous one.

In the anthropomorpic kabbalistic map of the human body, the *sefirah* of *yesod* is represented by the male sexual organ. I do not have space here to go into depth about the mysteries of sexual symbolism in the Kabbalah, and even raising the subject is fraught with the risk of misunderstanding. However, the idea of this correspondence is that the *sefirah* of *yesod* is the channel, or conduit through which the energies embodied in the higher *sefirot* flow into the world.

---

[5] Ibid.

The biblical character who embodies the attribute of *yesod* is Joseph. This connection is based on Joseph's mastery of his own sexuality, illustrated by his withstanding the temptation offered by Potiphar's wife. The Talmud (Sotah 36b) dramatically embellishes the event: Joseph was on the verge of succumbing to her blandishments, when he saw a vision of his father's face at the window. 'In future your brothers' names will be on the garments of the High Priest when he enters the Holy of Holies. Do you want to lose your place for the sake of a moment's pleasure?' demands the the vision. Faced with the fact that he will lose his connection to the Jewish past and future, Joseph desists.

Yesod corresponds to the sixth day of creation on which were created human beings, and the human ability to use our native powers for good or evil.

malkhut

Malkhut, which literally means 'kingship' (from *melekh*, king) is the last of the ten *sefirot*. As a receptacle at the level of our physical world, which absorbs the spiritual energies of the other *sefirot*, it symbolizes the power of receiving. *Malkhut* is conceived as having no particular colour or character of its own, but is formed by the lights of the other *sefirot* which pour into it.

Malkhut is so called because it is the *sefirah* through which God exercises direct influence in our world. Rabbi Aryeh Kaplan suggests a further reason. Malkhut is the *sefirah* through which God's light is most filtered and concealed. This concealment is what enables us to be co-creators in God's world. *Malkhut* makes possible true kingship; ability of the king's subjects to participate in their own governance.

Malkhut is also known as *shekhina* which is God's immanent presence in the world (deriving from *shokhen* meaning to neighbour or dwell). *Shekhina* is associated with the 'feminine' aspect of God which accompanies and comforts us whatever happens. (Talk of masculine and feminine aspects of God should not be rigidly tied to characteristics of actual men and women.)

The day of creation associated with *malkhut/shekhina* is Shabbat. After labouring physically and spiritually for six days, the rest of Shabbat allows us to receive, absorb and enjoy the fruits for which we have striven during the working week.

13

Spirituality

Some non-Jewish readers might be surprised at the words collected here under this title. Terms like mitzvah, halakhah *and* tikkun olam *describe action rather than communion or contemplation.*

However, deeds are the primary, though not exclusive, focus of Jewish spirituality. As a Buddhist friend of mine who grew up Christian put it, generalizing heroically, though not (in my humble opinion) falsely: 'Buddhism is most about what you are; Christianity is about what you believe; Judaism is about what you do'. Of course all three religions are concerned with believing, being and doing, but there is a question of emphasis.

In Judaism action is the fulcrum that transforms being. The Talmud asks, 'how can we walk after God? By visiting the sick, clothing the naked, burying the dead and comforting mourners (Sotah 14a).

Inner life is subject to flux and uncertainty. We can believe six impossible things before breakfast. We may be saintly and forbearing one moment but petty and grudging the next.

Mitzvah deeds crystallize this flow into a definite form and, over time, educate our inner lives towards goodness. As the nineteenth-century Rabbi Israel Salanter put it, 'meeting my neighbours' material needs is my spiritual need'.

ahavah

Ahavah means *love* in Hebrew. The Jewish mystics remark on the affinity between the word *ahavah*, love and *ehad*, one. The numerical value of their letters is the same: thirteen. Oneness, unity is the aspiration of love, and love emerges from a perception of unity. This insight is also expressed in the Shema prayer. The first line of Shema declares God's unity, and ends with the word *echad*. Then follows the *mitzvah* to love God. Love comes out of a sense of God's unity pervading all things.

There are three commands to love in the Torah: 'Love your neighbour as yourself' (Leviticus 19.18); 'Love the stranger as yourself, for you were strangers in Egypt' (Leviticus 19.34); and 'You shall love the Lord your God for all your heart, soul and strength' (Deuteronomy 6.4). The commentators are exercised by the question of how we can be commanded to feel an emotion such as love. Surely we either have it or we don't. The general answer is that indeed one cannot command feelings. The content of these *mitzvot* to love is do actions which will engender love. In the case of love of God, the point is to be in awe and amazement of God's creation. In the case of love for other people, the Torah is telling us to act lovingly – to go

164

and visit the person in hospital, give to charity, take out the rubbish, or change the baby's nappy – and that this will bring us to love.

avodah zarah

Avodah zarah is 'idolatry'. Literally it means, 'strange worship' or 'service'. The second of the Ten Commandments forbids making and worshipping idols. From the moment that the Jews entered the Land of Israel, the pagan cults of the surrounding peoples were a periodic source of temptation, against which the prophets warned and fought.

The rabbis compiled a whole Talmudic tractate about *avodah zarah*. Recognizing the dangers of being a small, exiled, monotheistic people living among predominantly idolatrous neighbours, they expanded the range of restrictions on contact with idolatry.

It was forbidden to gain any economic benefit from idolatrous worship, from the verse, 'Nothing of it shall stick to your hand' (Deuteronomy 13.18). This is the basis of the recent *sheitel* controversy, which has led to some authorities banning wigs made from hair cut in religious ceremonies in India. (I am not competent to judge the halakhic case for this, but one has to wonder about the investment of communal energy in this issue, when we are confronted with 50 per cent intermarriage, world hunger, an imminently nuclear-armed Iran and other such challenges.)

Colloquially, *avodah zarah* is used to describe anything

which is inappropriately worshipped, for example, money, dieting, your mobile phone, or David Beckham.

I hear that the new craze in New York and London is yoga classes for dogs. At the end, the dogs are encouraged to clasp their paws in a gesture of prayer. I'm not sure if the dog can be said to be engaged in *avodah zarah*, but it seems to me suspiciously like worshipping your dog.

egel hazahav

Egel hazahav, 'golden calf', is a phrase in modern Hebrew (which is full of bits and pieces of Bible and Midrash, in the same way as English contains unrecognized expressions from Shakespeare). You can hear it on the radio in the run-up to the Knesset elections: one candidate will describe another's values, policies or priorities as a golden calf, whether it's secularism or settlements.

The sense is of something like a totem or fetish bordering on, but not quite being, idolatrous in its importance to the opponent.

Interestingly, this usage reflects traditional discussions of the sin of the golden calf. The glaring question is: how could the Israelites have carried out this apparently idolatrous act immediately after experiencing God's revelation at Sinai? (A midrash compares it to a bride committing adultery the day after her wedding.)

While some commentators, including Rashi, are unsparing in their condemnation of the act as idolatrous, others, most prominently the twelfth-century thinker Rabbi

Yehudah Halevi, mitigate the crime. According to Halevi, the people didn't actually believe the calf to be a god, but succumbed to an understandable (though still problematic) human craving for something tangible and physical with which to approach God. (Hence, the sanctuary was a divinely sanctioned way of meeting this need.)

In this way, the nuance of Bible commentary supplies contemporary Hebrew with a phrase that conveys harsh criticism of a fixed idea, while stopping short of the charge of idolatry.

halakhah

Halakhah is usually translated as Jewish law. However, the word itself tells us that *halakhah* is much more than a legal system. It comes from the verb *holekh*, which means 'walk' or 'go'. *Halakhah* is the way Jews walk in the world; the spiritual path which is unique to us. The practices of *halakhah* permeate most aspects of life: business, family, everyday ethics, work, prayer and play, from car-pool to kitchen, bedroom to boardroom. There are *halakhot* about every stage of life and every core human experience.

Halakhah is not meant to be a desiccated, rule-bound pedantry, but a way to infuse even the most mundane moments with awareness of God and our role in the world. It helps us to keep sight of and live up to our highest ideals amidst the pressures and stresses of daily life.

The Torah tells us to walk (*holekh*) in God's paths and to 'go [*holekh*, again] after the Lord your G-d'

167

(Deuteronomy 13). The rabbis query how it is possible to walk after God who is, after all, utterly transcendent and beyond us (Talmud Sotah 14a). The answer they give is that we can walk in the paths of divine actions by visiting the sick, clothing the naked, burying the dead, comforting the suffering, etc. *Halakhah* is thus presented as the way in which we crystallize our inchoate yearnings to cleave to God into definite, human-scale ethical action.

heshbon nefesh

Taking a *heshbon nefesh* is one of the annual religious practices recommended. It means an 'accounting of the soul'. We examine the credit and debit columns of our spiritual lives: where we've made a profit, so to speak, and where a loss; where we've built up capital, and where we've depleted it.

With the balance sheet before us, we can draw up a viable business plan to stay spiritually solvent in the coming year.

Though it may seem incongruous, traditional sources frequently apply business metaphors such as *heshbon nefesh* to our spiritual lives. Pirkei Avot, the Ethics of the Fathers, advises us to weigh our actions carefully: 'Estimate the loss of a *mitzvah* against the reward, and the reward of a sin against the loss'. It expresses the urgency of life in this way: 'The day is short, the work is great, the workers are lazy, the payment is much, and the Boss is pressing'.

An example from American literature is the first chapter of *Walden*, in which Thoreau itemizes every cent he spent on the simple house he built, demonstrating the rigour of his life.

The point of these metaphors is to show the meticulousness and discipline with which we should approach our spiritual lives. For most people, nowhere is a more thorough and transparent accounting required than in their finances. Small items which are forgotten or overlooked can have serious consequences.

The Torah wants us to consider that on the Days of Awe an equally full and perspicuous account is required of our actions in the rest of our lives.

hisboddedus

Hisboddedus means 'making oneself alone'. It comes from the Hebrew word *bodded*, meaning alone, or singular. It's used to describe various Jewish spiritual and meditative practices which require solitude, and the quietening of distracting outside noise so that one can focus on communing with the divine.

Though the first mention of *hisboddedus* appears to be in Yosef Albo's fourteenth-century Sefer Ha'Ikkarim, the most enthusiastic practioners of *hisboddedus* are the Bratzlav Hasidim, who made it the cornerstone of their spiritual path.

In Bratzlav practice, *hisboddedus* means going to a secluded place, whether a private room or a Ukrainian forest and speaking to God, simply, honestly and directly, in your own words, and in whatever language you know best. You express hopes, desires, doubts before God as if you were talking to a friend. Rabbi Nachman of Bratzlav (1772–1810) recommended pouring out one's heart to God like this for an hour each day, then endeavouring to be joyful the rest of the time. (In our attention-deficient times, people I meet say they find it hard to do *hisboddedus* for more than 20 minutes.)

I am told that even today, if you live in Har Nof, a suburb on the edge of the Jerusalem Forest you can hear devoted Bratzlav Hasidim calling out to their Father in Heaven in the night.

kavod

Kavod (or *koved*) means 'honour', 'respect' or 'dignity' (also 'mass' or 'weight'). It is bestowed on distinguished rabbis by standing up before them and on substantial donors to worthy causes in numerous ways, but its uses in Jewish life are far more diverse.

Kavod Shabbat, 'respect for the Sabbath' is shown by bathing, dressing well and beautifying the house in its honour. *Kavod habriot*, 'respect for people', refers to the intrinsic dignity of human beings: it is a powerful halakhic concept, permitting some rabbinic commandments to be set aside when *kavod habriot* may otherwise be infringed.

Kavod hamet, 'respect for the dead', is behind the

Jewish emphasis on burying corpses swiftly and with the utmost dignity.

Kavod hatorah is the respect due to those who have made themselves one with the Torah's wisdom. *Kavod hashem*, God's *kavod*, is a mystical concept denoting God's presence as revealed in the world, as in 'the whole world is full of his *kavod*' (Isaiah 6.3).

Jewish tradition is adamant that *kavod* is gained not by seeking it, but by fleeing it.

Pirkei Avot, the Ethics of the Fathers, teaches, 'Who is honoured? [*m'khubad*]. One who honours others' (4.1). In a famous story, the student complains to his rabbi, 'I am trying to run from *kavod* but still I'm not getting any'. To which the rabbi replies, 'But maybe you are looking over your shoulder to see if it is following you?'

kiddush Hashem

The phrase means 'Sanctification of the Name'. It is most commonly known in the context of martyrdom. Jews who chose to die rather than convert, or to avoid committing murder, incest or idol-worship, are said to have died *al kiddush Hashem*.

Kiddush Hashem also covers Jews who are killed just because they are Jews, such as the victims of the Shoah. But Judaism is not a religion which seeks out martyrdom for its followers. 'You shall live by them [the *mitzvot*], not die by them', interpreted the rabbis (Sanhedrin 74a). But in extreme cases martyrdom is mandated as a testimony to the depth of Jews' commitment to Judaism.

Kiddush Hashem also has a broader meaning, for which nobody needs to die, and which any Jew can fulfil dozens of times a day. Any act we do which brings credit to Jews, Judaism and the God of Judaism in the eyes of onlookers is a *kiddush Hashem*. People have called Ilan Ramon a *kiddush Hashem*, because he was proudly Jewish in space, and used his few days of fame to exemplify what's best about us to billions.

More mundanely, if the cashier gives us too much change, and we return it (a small act but one which would astound and amaze most British shopkeepers today), that's a *kiddush Hashem*, too (if the cashier knows that we're Jewish).

We can achieve *kiddush Hashem* by speaking kindly, acting decently and doing business honestly. The more publicly we are identified as Jews, the greater the responsibility to be a *kiddush Hashem* in our actions, and not the opposite.

lifnim mishurat hadin

Those who see Judaism as a religion of law may be surprised to hear that the Jewish ideal is to act beyond the letter of the law (*lifnim mishurat hadin* in Hebrew, literally 'inside the line of law').

In a bold statement of this idea, Nachmanides (1194–1270) teaches that the laws of the Torah cannot legislate for more than a fraction of the ethical dilemmas we will face in life. However, through keeping the Torah we can fine-tune our moral sensibilities so that we will be able to intuit what's the right thing to do in cases that are not legislated and to do more than the Torah requires in situations that are. (Nachmanides on Deuteronomy 6.18, 'You shall do what is right and good in the eyes of God.')

The Talmud even considers the paradoxical possibility that going beyond the letter of *halakhah* is itself what the *halakhah* requires of us (Bava Metzia 83a).

In the period leading up to Rosh Hashanah we fear what might be the consequences if God were to judge us with precise justice untempered by compassion. In numerous places, the rabbis teach that if we behave towards others *lifnim mishurat hadin*, with generosity and kindness beyond what is strictly required, then we might hope that God will act *lifnim mishurat hadin* with us, and forgo the harshness that rigorous application of justice would require.

maggidim

The *maggidim* were a fixture on the Jewish landscape in prewar Europe. Itinerant preachers, parable-makers and story-tellers, they would wander from town to town, speaking and teaching in the market-places, educating, berating and inspiring their audiences.

The best were closely attuned to the spiritual needs of their public, yet fearless in criticizing them. Occasionally they became communal leaders, like the eighteenth-century Maggid of Mezirich, the Baal Shem Tov's successor as head of the Hasidic movement. Usually without any official position, *maggidim* functioned as a sort of non-establishment intelligentsia. Bloggers are probably the closest contemporary equivalent.

Maggid, which simply means 'one who tells' (related to the word *haggadah*), was also the name given to spirits who would appear to Jewish mystics and communicate secret teachings. These *maggidim* were a phenomenon among the kabbalists who flourished in Sefat from the sixteenth century.

The most famous *maggid* was the one who spoke regularly to Rabbi Yosef Caro (1488–1575), the author of the Shulhan Arukh, the Code of Jewish Law. As a rule, the *maggid* would appear to him early on Shabbat morning after Caro had studied several chapters of Mishnah.

The *maggid* would teach Caro kabbalistic secrets, berate him for eating and sleeping more than warranted by his usual ascetic discipline, offer words of personal support, and occasionally comfort him for the tribulations Caro suffered through the synagogue politics of Tzefat. One can read Caro's account of the *maggid*'s visitations in his book *Maggid Mesharim*.

makom

Makom means 'place'. A place humming with Jewish activity is known as a *makom Torah*.

If (heaven forbid) you should receive a disapproving frown when you sit down in *shul*, it may be that you have inadvertently occupied someone's *makom kavuah*, 'regular place'. (Of course, you should never receive, and still less give, disapproving frowns for any reason in *shul* ...)

A surprising and interesting use of the word *makom* is as a name of God. *Mitzvot* such as Shabbat and kashrut, which do not directly involve other people, are known as '*mitzvot being adam v'Makom*', *mitzvot* between people and God.

A traditional way of comforting mourners is to say '*HaMakom yenachem otcha*', 'May The Place [God] comfort you.'

The Midrash (Bereishit Rabbah 68.5) explains the insight behind this usage: 'He is the place of the world, and the world is not his place'. God is not found in any particular location; rather, God is immanent in all places.

Perhaps this explains why the word *makom* is used for God in the two examples above. *Mitzvot bein adam v'Makom* are not directed to a particular person but towards God who is omnipresent: the formula '*HaMakom yenachem*' reminds the mourner that God, the source of comfort, is not distant but may be found anywhere.

mikvah

Mikvah is one of the most important and neglected institutions of Jewish life. Jewish law considers building a *mikvah* to be a higher priority for a community than building a synagogue.

A *mikvah* is a pool of water which is built into the ground. Its contents must be rain water, or a natural river or spring, with a minimum volume of 200 gallons. The word *mikvah* means a 'gathering of water' and appears in the story of creation at the beginning of the Torah (Genesis 1.10).

The *mikvah* is an agent of purification. It is used principally for conversion and for keeping the laws of family purity (*niddah*). According to the *halakhah*, a married couple abstain from sexual relations during the woman's menstrual period, and for seven days afterwards. At the end of that time she goes to the *mikvah* and they resume intimacy. This rhythm of separation and reunification has the effect of constantly renewing their sexual bond, as well as making them relate on a non-physical level for nearly half of each month.

There is also a widespread custom of immersing in a *mikvah* on the eve of Yom Kippur as a sign of purity and repentance. At the end of Yoma, the tractate about Yom Kippur, the Mishnah declares 'Happy are you, Israel! ...Who purifies you? Your Father in heaven' (Yoma 85a). The Mishnah compares God, especially on Yom Kippur, to a *mikvah*. We can immerse ourselves in the purity of the day, and emerge clean.

mitzvah

In colloquial Jewish parlance, a *mitzvah* is any generic good deed. So one might say 'do a *mitzvah* and load up the dishwasher', or 'it's a *mitzvah* to throw out that mouldy tomato'. This common usage is both a distortion of the traditional meaning and a deep insight into Jewish spirituality.

Mitzvah means 'commandment'. There are 613 of them in the Torah, 248 do's and 365 don'ts. *Mitzvot* cover every aspect of life. Through them we can infuse all of existence with holiness.

It's a mark of Judaism that we relate to God primarily through actions, rather than through beliefs, emotions or silence (though they all have their role in Jewish spirituality). Through definite acts, our inchoate religious yearnings are crystallized into tangible forms of communal life.

Ibn Ezra points out that the root of the word *mitzvah* means 'connection'. Thus the *mitzvot* are also 613 opportunities to create a connection with God.

Our expansion of *mitzvah* to include any good deed comes from the Yiddish usage. A.J. Heschel suggests that it reflects an Eastern European Hasidic spirituality in which the whole world is filled with opportunities to connect to God: 'no place is devoid of his presence'.

Not just the 613 *mitzvot* of the Torah but every moment, place or person can offer such a chance. Our sense that there's a *mitzvah* to load the dishwasher contains an echo of that mystical worldview.

ness

Ness means 'miracle', but also 'flag' or 'banner'. Miracles and banners, on the face of it, do not appear to have any connection with one another. The fact that there is one Hebrew word for both sheds light on a deep Jewish understanding of the meaning of miracles.

A miracle is normally understood to be manifest divine intervention in the ordinary run of things. Sticks usually stay sticks. When they turn into snakes, we sit up and take notice. In this way, miracles flag up God's presence in the world. The ordinary run of things, the usually reliable correlations of cause and effect, are a veil concealing the divine nature of the everyday. Miracles momentarily lift the veil.

This helps us to understand an ancient and modern argument about Hanukah. What was the main miracle of the festival? Was it the improbable military victory of the few Hasmoneans against the mighty Greeks? Or was it the endurance of the single cruse of pure oil which was only enough for one day but which lasted for eight?

The Maharal of Prague has an interesting resolution. A military victory, however seemingly unlikely, can always be explained retrospectively by naturalistic means. The Hasmoneans were few, but maybe their superior tactics, training or motivation explain their triumph.

For the Maharal, the oil miracle signals the miracu-lousness of the whole story, including the victory of the few against the many, which we, in our rationalistic age, might be tempted to explain away.

selichah

Selichah is the closest word in Hebrew to 'excuse me'. Israelis used to mutter this as they elbowed past you in the bus queue. My impression is that now they are a bit more sombre and less abrasive in public spaces. Maybe this is to do with the statistically remote, but mentally ever-present, risks that fellow passengers know they are sharing.

Selichah literally means 'forgiveness'. We pray for it on Yom Kippur. We implore God to overlook our wrong-doings, in virtue of our *teshuvah*, *tefilah* and *tzedakah* (inadequately rendered as 'repentance, prayer and charity').

Full forgiveness involves not just not bearing a grudge for the past wrong but also restoring a damaged relationship to its former closeness.

Before Yom Kippur we try to cultivate a forgiving disposition. People ask each other for *'selichah* and *mechilah'* (another word for forgiveness), on account of the ways they may have hurt one another. If asked, it's a *mitzvah* to grant forgiveness.

In a famous and enigmatic story, the Hasidic rebbe Levi Yitzhak of Berditchev tells us that on Yom Kippur we need to forgive God also – to try to overcome the anger and pain that we may feel at the circumstances life has dealt us. 'I forgive You', he used to roar at the heavens, 'Now you, too, must forgive.'

shem

Shem, 'name', is a central idea in Judaism and crops up widely in common Jewish expressions. A *shem tov*, a good name, is the highest of spiritual crowns or attainments according to Pirkei Avot, the Ethics of the Fathers, 4.17. Ecclesiastes puns that a *shem tov* is better than good oil (*shemen tov*).

The founder of Hasidism, Israel Ben Eliezer (1698–1760), was known as the Baal Shem Tov, the Master of the Good Name. This appellation was also used of mystical rabbis before him and refers to mastery of the powers inherent in God's Ineffable Name.

In religious circles, God is often called *Hashem*, meaning 'The Name'. Since God is unknowable, we cannot say anything specific to refer to him. (Even calling him 'him' is taking a liberty.)

We cannot pronounce the names of God because of their great holiness, hence we simply say, 'The Name'. *Barukh Hashem*, meaning 'Blessed be the Name', is an answer to the question 'How are you?' It gives no specific information about one's situation, but conveys religious gratitude for whatever the situation is.

Lishma, meaning 'for the sake of the Name', is another important variant. To do something *lishma* means for the right reason, (i.e. out of a sincere desire to do the right thing, rather than with an eye on wealth, honour or prestige).

Good actions, even though performed not *lishma*, are

still better than nothing; the Talmud says, 'A person should anyway learn Torah and do *mitzvot* not *lishma*, because out of "not *lishma*", *lishma* will come' (Pesachim 50b).

sinat hinam

Sinat hinam means 'groundless hatred'. (The verb *soneh* means 'hate', as in the command *'lo tisnah at ahikha b'levavekha'*, do not hate your brother in your heart (Leviticus 19.17). *Hinam* comes from *hen* (grace). *Sinat hinam* is therefore hatred that is *gratis*. It refers to the internecine strife which is unfortunately too common in Jewish communities whether between Reform and Orthodox, Ashkenazim and Sephardim, the rabbi and the *hazan*, the president of the *shul* and the board. You could charitably ascribe its existence to the high stakes decisions that Jewish communites have had to make, or to a persecuted people internalizing the hatred directed at them, and then projecting it against other groups of Jews. Either way, there is clearly too much of it about.

The Talmud already knew of the phenomenon, and its destructive effect on Jewish life. Yoma 9b records that the First Temple was burned down because of idol worship, sexual immorality and bloodshed. At the time of the Second Temple's destruction, on the other hand, the Jews were pious, but the Temple was lost because *sinat hinam*, groundless hatred, was endemic to Jewish national life. From this the Talmud infers that groundless hatred is as

181

grave as idol worship, sexual immorality and bloodshed put together.

Rabbi Abraham Isaac Kook, first Chief Rabbi of Israel, famously wrote that if the Second Temple was destroyed and the people scattered through *sinat hinam* (groundless hatred), then the Temple will be rebuilt and the people gathered together again through *ahavat hinam* (causeless love).

tikkun olam

Probably the snappiest mission statement for the Jewish people occurs in the second paragraph of the Aleinu prayer: *l'takken olam b'malkhut shaddai*: to mend the world under the sovereignty of God. This phrase reflects two deep Jewish ideas. First, the world is imperfect and broken. There is suffering and injustice. God calls us to partnership in the work of fixing this fractured world. Second, this striving towards justice takes place under the sovereignty of God. Our work in *tikkun olam* points people towards a knowledge of *malkhut shaddai* – the God who commands us to repair and heal.

Imperfection in the created world is a distinctive theme in traditional sources. A famous midrash has Rabbi Akiva asking Tornus Rufus, the Roman governor, which is better; a bundle of wheat or a loaf of bread? 'The wheat, of course', Tornus Rufus replies. 'Precisely', says Rabbi Akiva. The bread is the product of our perfection of the wheat, which is given by God.

In the kabbalistic theosophy, brokenness and fragmentation are consequences of the primal act of creation. Divine light is poured into 'vessels' which are unable to bear the intensity of the influx and shatter. The human work of *tikkun* is to repair the vessels and gather up the scattered fragments of light.

In recent decades, *tikkun olam* has come to refer to any religiously motivated action towards social justice, whether environmental activism, working for third world development, or rights for the disabled. In this way, the sphere of Jewish responsibility is broadened to encompass aspiring to fix the toughest socio-economic problems.

tzedakah

Tzedakah is fulfilled by giving to the needy. It does not mean charity: rather, the root of *tzedakah* is *tzedek*, which means justice. People with more ought to help people with less not out of beneficent feelings but because it is just and right to do so.

Maimonides writes that we should be more careful about doing *tzedakah* than about any other positive *mitzvah*, and that helping each other is a particularly Jewish trait. (Not that other peoples can't help each other too.) He even says that if someone is hard-hearted and doesn't help other people, there's cause to doubt his Jewish lineage.

The *halakhah* details how to do this important *mitzvah*. We should give 10–20 per cent of our income *tzedakah*, depending on our means. If we are exceptionally rich we may give more. We should try to make sure that we give to genuinely needy recipients and through reliable agents, but if a person is hungry we should give without checking. Most say that we should give at least a small amount to a beggar on the street; whether or not they are deserving we don't want to accustom ourselves to callousness. Ordinarily, our first responsibility is to those closest to us, but we should feed the non-Jewish poor together with the Jewish poor.

Around the Days of Awe when we seek God's compassion we are told particularly to act with compassion towards others. Very few of us actually deserve God's mercy as of right, but by acting mercifully towards others whether deserving or not, we may merit it more.

tzelem Elohim

Tzelem Elohim means the 'image of God'. It's a phrase you hear a lot these days in the context of discussions about Jewish ethics. The Torah's claim that humans are created in God's image (Genesis 1.27) underlies Judaism's insistence that each and every person has infinite dignity and value by virtue of the divine image that he or she bears.

From this follows the requirement to treat every person with respect. Even a convicted murderer must be treated with dignity in the execution of his punishment (Talmud Sanhedrin 46a); he is still in the image of God.

The phrase is so common that it's easy to overlook its strangeness. What can it mean to say that we are made in the image of God when God, being invisible and incorporeal, has no image? Most of the great Jewish thinkers picked up on this problem, and gave a range of answers. Here are just two of them.

Maimonides, the greatest Jewish philosopher, asserted that our *tzelem Elohim* consists in our capacity for rational thought (Guide for the Perplexed, 1.1). Elsewhere (Laws of Repentance, Chapter 5), he implies that our likeness to the divine resides in our capacity to make moral distinctions between good and bad (based on Genesis 3.22.)

The Zohar, the classic of Jewish mysticism takes another view. It suggests that our likeness to God rests in our capacity for creativity (Zohar 1.15b). Just as God created and continues to create new and unprecedented things, so we are able also to form objects, thoughts, ideas, which are unique and original.

14

How is it in Hebrew?

Shortly before this book was completed (in 2006), Israel overtook the USA as home to the world's largest concentration of Jews. Israel's Jewish population is growing as the diaspora's ages and shrinks.

The centrality of Israel in Jewish life has brought a plethora of modern Hebrew words into everyday usage. Knesset and shalom *are often in the news. The Zionist youth movements and their successful post-high school year programmes have brought terms of art such as* shaliach *and* madrich *back to diaspora communities.*

Secular Zionism was a breathtakingly audacious attempt to recast some of the basic concepts of Jewish tradition in its own ideological mould. The effort was quite self-conscious in its use of language. Aliyah *which referred to spiritual elevation, or to the honour of being called up to the Torah, became the word for immigration to Israel.* Shaliach *which traditionally meant a messenger sent out to perform a* mitzvah *was now used to describe the Jewish Agency's sandal-wearing emissaries of the State of Israel to diaspora communities. Zionism pruned away the religious connotations of classical phrases and set them to work for new purposes. Ancient words, which, to the Zionists bespoke passivity and helplessness, were mobilized for a people once again taking its fate into its hands.*

There are those who regret this historical turn. For intellectuals such as George Steiner, powerlessness is the proper state of the Jewish people. To Steiner, statehood has diminished the fructifying power of cosmopolitan rootlessness. Contemporary efforts to revive Yiddish are motivated, at least in part, by ambivalence or hostility towards Zionism. These attempts seem to me poignant but futile. There is much that's appealing about the lost Yiddish culture of Eastern Europe: its self-deprecation, sensitivity to the shades of human misfortune and wry gallows humour. But in these very features it bears witness to the perils of Jewish powerlessness. The exercise of power comes with opposite dangers. For most Jews, however, they are decidedly better than the alternative.

aliyah

Aliyah means 'going up'. In the Torah we receive the *mitzvah* to go to Jerusalem for the three festivals of Pesach, Shavuot and Sukkot (Deuteronomy 16.16). The Mishnah in Hagigah 1.1 calls this *aliyah l'regel*, which means 'going up by foot'. (For most of us now, it is by plane.)

Aliyah l'regel was a literal ascent, to one of the highest places in Israel, and a spiritual ascent – to the holiest place in the world. Being called to read from the Torah is called getting an *aliyah* (Talmud, Megillah 23a). Whatever the topography of the synagogue, making the blessings over the Torah and reading from it, or following while someone else reads, represent a spiritual ascent.

Immigrating to Israel is called 'making *aliyah*'. This is not just a smart marketing ploy of the Jewish Agency. For many halakhic authorities, it is a positive *mitzvah* to live in Israel, unless there are overwhelming reasons not to. (The relative scarcity of Cadbury's chocolate in Israel does not count).

Moving to Israel enables one to live a more whole and fulfilled Jewish life, without the anxiety of perpetually feeling an outsider, which is characteristic of diaspora life.

Whatever the undoubted difficulties of living in Israel now, it's an opportunity to participate in the historic unfolding of the Jewish people's renewal in its land and the building of a Jewish country of which we may all be proud. On a personal note, my family and I were privileged to make *aliyah* in August 2003.

galut

Galut means 'exile'. It is used to describe the condition of living outside the Land of Israel, implying that such an existence is abnormal for the Jewish people. It has connotations of wandering, homelessness, fear and insecurity. It describes a temporary aberration, which will eventually be repaired by coming home.

In the three weeks preceding Tisha b'Av, we mark the destruction of the Temple and the scattering of the Jews of Israel which precipitated this current, prolonged episode of *galut*. We remind ourselves that it is not the natural or permanent state of the Jewish people.

The mystics also speak of *galut hashechinah*, the 'exile of God's presence from the Land', which coincided with the physical exile of the Jewish people. The *Shechinah* accompanies the Jews in their wandering, comforting them and empathetically sharing the pain of exile, in a way that is prefigured in the verse 'I am with him in his suffering' (Isaiah 43).

A further, mystical twist on the concept was the kabbalistic notion of *galut hadibbur*, the 'exile of speech'. The idea is that the travails of exile repress the ability of speech even to give expression to the full sorrow of our situation, or to our hopes for improvement, or to our full identity as Jews.

This notion has its roots in the Egyptian exile. The Jewish people sigh out of their slavery when Pharaoh dies, implying that before, they were unable even to sigh. Only when things improved a little, could they give expression to their condition.

geulah

Geulah, meaning redemption or deliverance, is what we celebrate on Pesach. On the last days of Pesach we especially mark the redemption of Israel from the Egyptian armies at the Red Sea.

Literally *ga'al* means to cover or protect (see Job 3.4).

(*Galut*, 'exile', the opposite of *geulah*, comes from the root meaning to uncover. *Galut* is the uncovering, or denuding, of the land of Israel of its inhabitants.)

Geulah also refers to the ransoming or redeeming of property that used to be yours. (The English word 'redemption' also has this dual financial and spiritual meaning). In the Pesach story, the redemption of Israel is God's recovering of the Jewish people after they had been alienated, spiritually and physically, under Egyptian servitude. Physically, the Jews had been slaves to foreign rulers. Spiritually, many had fallen under the spell of idolatry. *Geulah* refers to liberation both from alien masters and from strange gods.

Among Jews who hope avidly for the Messianic era, you often hear the wish expressed that we will all soon see the *geulah shleimah*, the complete redemption. The messianic redemption in the future is understood to be the Pesach liberation from false tyrannies of the body and the spirit writ large (Talmud Berachot 13a).

hafsakah

A *hafsakah* is a 'pause, break' or 'interval'. Despite recent efforts at public-sector reform in Israel, *hafsakah* is still where the government bureaucrat whom you need to see is quite likely to be.

On the eve of a fast-day, *hafsakah* is the term for the moment at which it is forbidden to eat or drink. On the eve of Pesach, it is the time when *hametz* is off-limits.

The root of the word is *psak*, which means to 'cut, break' or 'sever'. Numerous words and phrases come from it. A *psak halakhah* is a Jewish legal decision, so called because it cuts the complex skein of argument stretching through the Talmud and commentaries in order to give a clear, definite answer for a particular time and place.

A *posek* is a rabbi who is recognized as possessing the learning and authority needed to give a *psak halakhah*.

Among other cognate forms, a *psik* in Hebrew is a comma, and a Pesek Zman (Time Out) is the name of a chocolate bar which is similar to a Twix.

Hafsakah is not related to *hakafah*, the circling of the synagogue seven times with dancing and *sifrei Torah* which we do on Simchat Torah to celebrate ending and rebeginning the Torah. *Hakafah* comes from *makif*, which means to 'surround' or 'encompass'.

Our current custom is medieval in origin, though it is related to the practice of circling the altar with palms and willows in the Temple.

halutz

'In the days of the *halutzim*' is an expression one often hears in Israel. It evokes images of young people in shorts draining swamps, planting oranges and dancing the *hora* after a day's work in the fields.

Halutzim are pioneers, those who lead the way. After the Russian pogroms of 1881, a movement arose encouraging young people to move to what was then

Palestine to cultivate the land and prepare the way for the less robust populations to make *aliyah* later on. This movement was called 'Hechalutz', the pioneer.

One of the first appearances of the word *halutz* in the Bible is when the tribes of Reuben, Gad and half of Menasseh offer to lead the conquest of Canaan as *halutzim* (Numbers 32.17).

In the battle of Jericho, Joshua ordered *halutzim* to march before the priests (Joshua 6.7). In this case, *halutzim* denotes not only vanguard but also armed soldiers. *Halutz* has other meanings as well, including to rescue. The Psalmist thanks God '*Ki hilatztah nafshi mimavet*', (You have delivered me from death) (Psalm 116.8).

The young Russian Zionists post-1881 perhaps had all these meanings in mind, a vanguard ready to defend itself if necessary and seeking to rescue European Jewry from violent anti-Semitism.

Although Israel is no longer a malaria-ridden back-water, Israel and world Jewry still need their *halutzim* to face today's challenges.

hasbarah

Hasbarah is normally translated as 'PR' – public relations. These days, it's most frequently used in the context of anguished or scornful discussions about why Israeli spokespeople don't seem to convey their message very effectively.

I have no wish to pronounce on the success or otherwise of their sincere and dedicated efforts. However, thinking about the meaning and origin of the word can perhaps suggest different ways to communicate Israel's case to the world.

The modern Hebrew word *hasbarah* means 'explanation'. I heard communications trainer Neil Lazarus say that 'the problem with *hasbarah* is *hasbarah*' – all the interminable explanations.

A Palestinian on the radio claims: 'They're occupying our land and killing our children'. The Israeli counters: 'Let me explain: in 1947 the UN recommended a partition plan ...' As true as it all is, there's no question about who will receive a better hearing in our attention-deficient culture.

But the earlier connotation of the verb *l'hasbir* means 'to brighten', 'illuminate' or 'make clear'. When we do this to a concept or idea, we explain. We can also illuminate or brighten a face, or somebody else's.

Pirkei Avot, the Ethics of the Fathers, tells us to greet everybody *b'sever* (the same root as *hasbarah*) *panim yafot*, which means with a 'bright' or 'cheerful countenance'. Maimonides comments on this that we should try to speak to everyone pleasantly and calmly.

A friendly face and an affable manner can be better *hasbarah* than even the most cogent explanations.

LET'S SCHMOOZE: JEWISH WORDS TODAY

l'shanah haba'ah b'Yerushalayim

'*L'shanah haba'ah b'Yerushalayim*' (Next year in Jerusalem) is what we proclaim at the end of the Pesach Seder (as well as at the end of Yom Kippur).

It is not, primarily, the expression of a preferred destination for the following Pesach holiday, equally replaceable by Eilat, Tenerife or Hendon. Many *hagadot* add the word *habnuyah*, 'rebuilt', to the end of the phrase. We're hoping for a rebuilt Temple and the re-institution of *aliyah l'regel*, the mass pilgrimage of the Jewish people to Jerusalem on the three 'foot' festivals of Pesach, Shavuot and Sukkot (Deuteronomy 16.16).

Historians estimate that 100,000 visitors converged on Jerusalem every Pesach at the end of the Second Temple period, almost doubling the local population. (Today you can tour the infrastructure supporting that mass influx, which archaeologists have uncovered in the Ophel Gardens near the Temple Mount.)

It is also a straightforward expression of the centuries-long Jewish dream to return to the Land of Israel. Our ancestors, who annually declared their faithfulness to that dream, might have had a hard time understanding Jews who today have the opportunity freely to fulfil it but who decide that they would rather not.

Finally, it is a hope for a better future for the Jewish people and the whole world. We pray that the utopian turn history took with the exodus from Egypt continues

194

and completes itself through the dawning of an age of universal peace and freedom.

madrich

Madrich, according to the dictionary, means guide, trainer, educator. It can also be a guidebook, or a telephone directory.

In the world of Jewish youth movements, a *madrich* is a youth leader. The word also has the connotations of role model, inspiration and general font of wisdom. The *madrich* not only leads and runs tours, camps and programmes, but also inducts his or her charges (*hanichim*) into the ideology and mythology of the movement.

The craft of a *madrich* is known as *hadrakha*. Literally meaning 'leadership', this refers to the blend of charisma, educational nous and personal example which make a good *madrich*. *Hadrakha* also includes the *madrich*'s repertoire of tools and skills such as candle-lit sharing circles, and an immense collection of ice-breaking or mood-altering games, most of which seem to involve ping-pong balls. Good *hadrakha* requires striking a delicate balance between authority and mateyness; knowing when to break up the shaving-foam fight and when to join in.

Madrich and *hadrakha* both derive from *derekh*, meaning 'route', 'path', or 'way of life', as in 'you shall teach them the *derekh* in which they shall go' (Exodus 18.20).

195

Derekh, in turn, comes from the verb *darakh*, meaning to step or tread.

shaliach

When I was growing up, every youth movement had a *shaliach*. They were all kibbutzniks in sandals with heavily accented English. At the end of any programme, regardless of the content, they would stand up and urge us to go and live in *'Eeezzzra-el'*. (And here I am. Something obviously rubbed off.)

The root of *shaliach* is the verb *shalach* which means 'send'. A *shaliach* is an emissary or a messenger; one who is sent to fulfil a particular task. The *parsha* of *shalach lecha* begins with God's command to Moses, in those words, to send men on a mission to reconnoitre the Land of Israel (Bamidbar 13.2).

In *halakhah*, certain religious actions may be done on one's behalf via a *shaliach*. For example, one may appoint a *shaliach* to give a wedding-ring to your wife, or to deliver a bill of divorce. In general though, there is a principle that it is preferable to perform a *mitzvah* oneself rather than through a *shaliach*.

In Hasidic thought, the concept of *shaliach* is enlarged to encompass one's whole mission in life. Each of us is sent into the world with a *shlichut*, a mission which only we can carry out. There is no higher service than to figure out what is our unique *shlichut* in life, and to fulfil it.

shalom

From assimilated Jews to rickshaw-drivers in Kathmandu, *shalom* is the only Hebrew word many people know. It means 'peace', and also 'hello' and 'goodbye'.

The equivalence of these words in Hebrew is taken by many to show the centrality of peace in Judaism. Indeed, peace is a pervasive yearning in Jewish life and liturgy. The Amidah, recited thrice daily, ends with a plea for peace, and the Mishnah describes *shalom* as a vessel which can receive all blessings; without it, other good things cannot be preserved or enjoyed.

In the Bible, *shalom* usually means 'wholeness' or 'well-being', rather than the absence of conflict. So, Jacob asks Joseph to ascertain the *shalom* of his brothers, and of their sheep. *Shalom* is a state of harmony and flourishing of the good, which can sometimes be achieved only through victory over evil-doing nations. Isaiah's messianic vision of the wolf lying down with the lamb is juxtaposed with prophecy about the defeat of nations which have tormented Israel.

Shalom in Jewish sources also differs from the notion of peace as an achieved, static condition between conflicting parties. In Jewish tradition, peace is dynamic, something strived towards but never fully achieved in this world. The Talmud (Berachot 64a) tells us that we should part from a friend with the words '*lekh l'shalom*', (go towards peace), rather than '*lekh b'shalom*', (go in peace). The latter suggests a fully realized state of peace; the former expresses our aspiration towards ever higher levels of spiritual well-being, which is the essence of existence.

Zionism

These days, an Internet search of the word 'Zionism' is apt to suggest that it is a racist, fascist, imperialist, colonialist ideology ... Not very instructive.

Zionism is in fact the movement working for Jewish self-government in the Land of Israel, and since 1948, for developing the State of Israel.

The term was coined in 1886 by Nathaniel Birnbaum in his journal *Selbstemanzipation*, although the idea was expressed earlier in the nineteenth century. (See the novels of Disraeli and George Eliot's *Daniel Deronda*.) Birnbaum defined Zionism as the political movement for Jewish autonomy in the Land of Israel, in contradistinction to the Hibbat Zion organization, which promoted Jewish settlement in Israel without a political agenda.

The idea was more fully developed in 1896 by Theodor Herzl in his book *Der Judenstaat* (*The Jewish State*). Herzl argued tht increasing anti-Semitism made it imperative that the Jews should have their own state.

Originally, 'Zion' was the name for one of the hills of Jerusalem, which later became known as the City of David. The meaning of Zion is unclear; it may mean 'rock, stronghold', or 'dry place'. In the Bible, Zion became an expression for Jerusalem, and the Land of Israel as a whole.

In particular, it became the designation for the object of yearning when Jews longed for their homeland from exile, as in 'By the Rivers of Babylon, there we sat down; yea we wept, when we remembered Zion' (Psalm 137.1).

The poet Yehudah Halevi (1075–1141) also picks up this trope in his lament, 'Zion, won't you ask how your captives are?' The association of Zion with longing for Jerusalem made it a fitting name for the modern Zionist movement, dedicated to returning the Jewish people to their land.

Index

Yiddish and Hebrew words and expressions are in *italics* unless they are proper nouns (for example, festivals or sacred texts) or in common international circulation (for example, chutzpah, bar mitzvah). Several other major words, especially the Jewish festivals, do not have an section of their own, however they do appear in several sections.

INDEX

INDEX